着物と日本の色　子ども着物篇

Child Kimono and the colors of Japan

Kimono Collection of Katsumi Yumioka

編・コレクション　弓岡勝美

監修　藤井健三

はじめに

　本書では、宮参りから十三参りまでの「子ども時代の着物」を紹介いたします。子どもの着物の中には、大人の着物にはない楽しくて華やかな色柄がたくさん見られます。その愛らしい世界を、四季折々の自然の表情が感じられる色文様、子どもに関わりの深い季節の行事を交えてお伝えします。また健やかな成長を願って施された意匠や様式、服飾小物など、子どもの着物特有の世界も儀式の解説を交えてご紹介致します。

　本書でご覧いただける着物は江戸末期から昭和中期にかけてつくられたものです。古典的な文様を可愛らしく、そして大胆にアレンジした当時のセンスは、新鮮で斬新。図柄も玩具や童話、故事成語から構成されたもの、当時流行したキャラクター、戦中時ならではの図案など驚きのある物も残っています。その時代背景が如実に写し取られているのも子どもの着物特有の面白さ。さらに子どもの小さな身体に合わせて肩幅や着丈を調節された可愛らしいスケール感、躍動感も見所の一つです。

　四季の色の章では着物の中の色や紋意匠を四季毎に構成しましたが、そもそも着物や帯には様々な色や季節が複合されており、四季別に分けることは難しい部分もあります。本書では日本人が古来より親しんできた四季の花木の色をもとに、あくまでイメージとして分類しました。また文様についても絵画的にとらえて構成しています。古い着物の中にある色や文様をグラフィカルな視点からご覧いただくことで、皆さんの創造力を刺激できる内容を目指しました。

　皆様が初めて目にされるような色や柄、意匠でもその根底にあるのは子どもの健やかな成長を祈った親の願いです。成長の節目毎に特有の衣装を身につけさせ健やかな成長を願う、日本人が古から備えている子どもを大切にする文化も本書を通じて感じ取っていただけるよう願ってやみません。

　最後に、本書では紹介しきれなかった帯や着物がまだまだございます。またご紹介できることを楽しみにしています。

弓岡勝美

Introduction

This book is an introduction to kimono worn in childhood, from an infant's first shrine visit to the shrine visit at the age of 13. Children's kimono use many playful, vivid colors and motifs not found on kimono for adults. The charming world they present communicates to us the seasonal observations with which children were deeply connected, through colors and motifs that give a rich feel for the expression of each of the four seasons. This book also introduces the designs and styles used to express prayers for children's health and growth as well as the accessories children used, with explanations of the rituals and other aspects unique to the world of children's kimono.

The kimono presented in this book date from the late Edo through the mid Showa periods (approximately 1840 to 1960). The design sense employed in them, lovingly and boldly rearranging classic motifs, is fresh and innovative. Surviving works full of design surprises include designs composed with references to toys, legendary tales,Å@idiomatic phrases, popular characters, even designs only possible during the war years. One of the fascinating aspects of children's kimono is how faithfully they communicate the social context. Their charming scale, adjusted to fit the height and breadth of small bodies, and their vivid sense of energy further boost their appeal.

The chapter on seasonal colors presents the colors and design motifs used in kimono for each of the four seasons. Essentially, though, multiple colors and seasons merge in kimono and obi; categorizing them strictly by the seasons is difficult. To give a general impression of how the colors were used, however, this work classifies them in terms of the colors of the flowers and plants of the four seasons that have been an intimate part of Japanese lives throughout the ages. Similarly, the design motifs are organized on a pictorial basis. We hope that looking at the colors and designs used in old kimono from a graphic design point of view will stimulate your own creativity. The colors, motifs, and designs that you may be seeing here for the first time all carry, at root, a parent's prayer that the child wearing the kimono will grow up strong and healthy. The custom of having children don special clothing at the critical junctures in their growth stems from that same prayer, an expression of how dearly children have always been cherished in Japanese culture. We hope that this book will give a sense not only of the creativity and sense of style that went into designing children's kimono but also of the love that inspired them.

Please note that were able to introduce only a small subset of these kimono and obi in this book. We look forward to following it with additional fascinating volumes introducing these delightful works.

Katsumi Yumioka

Child Kimono and the colors of Japan
Kimono Collection of Katsumi Yumioka

Collection ©2007 Katsumi Yumioka
Published by PIE BOOKS

PIE BOOKS
2-32-4, Minami-Otsuka, Toshima-ku, Tokyo 170-0005 JAPAN
Tel: +81-3-5395-4811 Fax: +81-3-5395-4812
e-mail: editor@piebooks.com   sales@piebooks.com
http://www.piebooks.com
ISBN 978-4-89444-607-6
Printed in Japan

着物と日本の色　子ども着物篇
Child Kimono and the colors of Japan

もくじ
Contents

春 Spring 15-49

夏 Summer 55-89

秋 Autumn 97-127

冬 Winter 129-159

儀式と着物 Kimono & Ceremonies 161-185

着物の文様 Pattern 191-235

本書の着物とその色名の組み合せにつきましては、
一部の着物のイメージを考慮して実際の色とは多少異なる場合がございます。ご了承下さい。

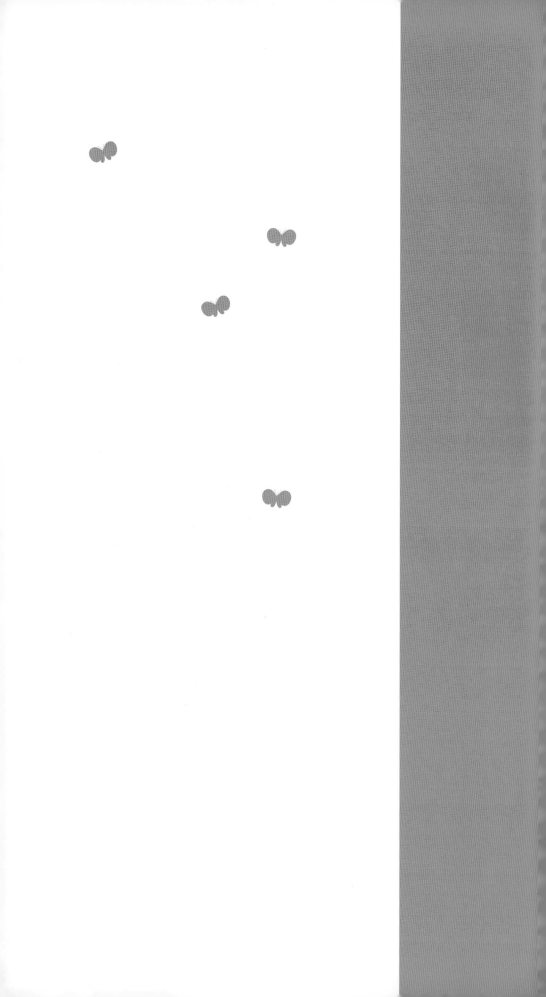

雪もまだ消えやらぬうちに樹々草々は
目ざめの季節を迎える。春である。萌
え出づる新芽、若葉は、柔毛に覆われ
るもの、赤みを帯びるもの、緑はまだ色
も幼い。葉に先立ち咲きだす花々も色
は淡い。これが早春の色である。やが
て花色は、黄、赤、紫に濃いみを増し、
葉は艶の緑に移る。春たけなわ、生命
溢れる季節の色といえるだろう。

Spring is when the trees and grasses
start to wake, even before the snow
melts. The light green of fresh, downy
young leaves, as well as the soft colors
of the flowers that bloom before the
leaves bud, are the typical tones of
early spring. The yellow, red, and
purple hues of the flowers then
thicken, as the leaves turn to a glossy
green. The colors of spring convey all
of the abundant energy of life.

庭梅色

Niwaume iro

にわうめ

明るく薄い赤色。やわらかい淡紅色である鴇（とき）色を浅くした色ともいえる。庭梅は江戸時代に中国から伝わったバラ科の鑑賞用低木で漢名は「郁李（いくり）」。4月、やや桜に遅れて、葉に先だって鮮やかな淡紅色の五弁花を咲かせる。八重咲きのものは特に「庭桜（にわざくら）」ともよばれる。7月に光沢のある実をつけ、熟すと食べられる。

Niwa-ume iro is a light faint red, lighter than *toki-iro* (carnation-pink; *toki* is a Japanese crested ibis). *Niwaume* (garden plum) is an ornamental rosaceous shrub (*yuli* in Chinese), imported from China in the Edo period. This plant bears five-petaled, bright pink flowers before its leaves bud, and comes into full bloom following the cherry blossoms in April. A double-petaled type of *niwa-ume*, also known as *niwa-zakura* (Japanese garden cherry), bears shiny, edible cherries in July.

三葉躑躅色

Mitsuba-tsutsuji iro

みつばつつじ

やや黄色がかった薄い赤紫。あざやか
な赤紫の躑躅色より気持ち品がある色
合といえるかもしれない。三葉躑躅は
ツツジ科のうちの三枚葉を輪生させる
一群で、山地に多く、3月下旬から4月
上旬にかけて他の躑躅に先立って花を
咲かせるので「一番躑躅」の名がある。
葉の出る前に枝一杯に鮮やかな花を
つけるので、葉とともに花を咲かせる
通常の躑躅にもまして愛でる人も多い。

This is a light, slightly yellowish red-
purple, more refined than *tsutsuji iro* (a
bright red-purple, the color of azalea).
Mitsuba-tsutsuji is a clover-like
ericaceous plant, particularly common
in mountainous areas. This flower is
called the "first azalea" because it
blooms earlier than other azaleas,
from the end of March to early April.
Mitsuba-tsutsuji appeals to many for the
bright bunches of flowers that emerge
before the leaves bud; this variety is
thus more striking and popular than
other azaleas, whose flowers bloom
along with their leaves.

山吹色

Yamabuki iro

やまぶき

支子（くちなし）の実を染料にした赤みがかった黄色。濃黄の鬱金（うこん）よりやや赤みが強い。山吹はバラ科の落葉低木で、4月、桜の終わるころ葉陰に楚々とした一重の花を咲かせるので、春の終わりを飾る花として万葉の昔から日本人に愛されてきた。平安貴族の襲（かさね）の色目の重要色で、『源氏物語』では、光源氏が見初めた幼い紫の上は山吹襲の表着姿であった。ちなみに山吹色は黄金色と同じに用いられ、江戸時代には大判・小判の比喩となった。

This is a reddish yellow dyed with gardenia fruit, slightly more reddish than turmeric yellow. *Yamabuki* is a deciduous rosaceous shrub, bearing modest single blossoms hidden behind its leaves in April, just after the cherry blossoms. The plant has been beloved as a symbol of the end of spring since the period of the Anthology of Ten Thousand Leaves. This color was an important one in the aristocratic kimono color scheme of the Heian period. In the Tale of Genji, young *Murasaki-no-ue* wore *yamabuki* kimono on her first meeting with *Hikaru-genji*. *Yamabuki iro* sometimes refers to the color of gold and was used as a metaphor for gold coins in the Edo period.

やや緑がかった黄色。緑みの黄の黄蘗（きはだ）より気持ち浅い色。畑一面に黄色い十字花を咲かせる菜の花は春の盛りの風物詩ともいえ、小学唱歌『朧月夜』、山村暮鳥の詩のリフレイン「いちめんのなのはな、いちめんのなのはな…」を思い出させる。江戸時代以前からの色名に「菜種色」というものもあったが、こちらは菜種油の色のことらしい。

Greenish yellow, slightly lighter than *kihada-iro*. The color of *nanohana*(rape blossoms). The yellow ocean of this plant's cruciate flowers evokes a typical spring landscape and reminds Japanese people of "*oboro-zukiyo*," celebrated songs for schoolchildren, as well as poetry by *Bocho Yamamura*, inspired by carpets of field mustard. Field mustard was also used in the name of the color *natane iro* before the Edo period, but this phrase seems more to have referred to the color of rapeseed oil, instead of the yellow hue of the flowers.

菜の花色

Nanohana iro

なのはな

早蕨色

Sawarabi iro

さわらび

灰がかって青みをもつ薄緑。くすんだ青緑の木賊（とくさ）色を薄くした色といってもよいだろう。蕨は山地・草原にふつうに見られるシダ科の植物で、早春、こぶし状に巻いた新葉を出し、これを特に早蕨という。原産する野菜の乏しかった日本では古代から食べられてきた山野草で、若葉を叩き蕨、お浸し、天麩羅にして賞味する。根茎からは澱粉が採れ蕨餅の原料となる。『源氏物語』は「早蕨」の帖名を設け、「蕨、つくづくし、をかしき籠に入れて」と語られている。

This is a grayish Nile green, similar to *tokusa iro* (the color of scouring rushes), but even lighter. *Warabi* (a kind of fern) is common in mountains and fields, and its young fiddlehead frond, which emerges in early spring, is called *sawarabi*. This was an important food source in ancient Japan, where few native vegetables were available. People still enjoy eating marinated or boiled *warabi*, or fried as tempura. *Warabi* starch is used for *warabi-mochi* (sweet dumplings). One of the chapters in Tale of Genji was titled *Sawarabi*, and the story mentions *warabi* and field horsetail.

枝垂柳色

Shidare-yanagi iro

しだれやなぎ

明るく、やや黄みがかった緑。本来の
柳色は新芽の色をいい、この色よりや
わらかくくすんでいる。私たちは柳とい
うとまず枝垂柳をイメージするが、日本
にある約90種の柳のうちの1種のみで
他の柳は枝垂れない。古くから新緑の
美しさ、水辺の風にたゆたう姿が愛さ
れ、素性法師の「見渡せば柳桜をこき
まぜて…」とあるように平安京の都大路
に街路樹として植えられていた。

Shidare-yanagi iro is a bright yellowish
green, softer and dimmer than *yanagi
iro* (the color of fresh leaves).
Weeping willow is most famous of the
willows, but in fact, it is only one of
some 90 different kinds of willows in
Japan–the remaining willows don't
necessarily 'weep,' dropping their
branches. Beautiful green willow
branches of all types, swaying in the
wind, have been loved through the
ages; willow trees lined the streets of
the ancient capital of *Heian-Kyo*
(ancient Kyoto), as recounted in the
poetry of the priest *Sosei*.

やや赤みがかった薄茶。紅梅の根を煎じた梅屋渋で染めた梅染（うめぞめ）色に近い。土筆はシダ植物スギナの胞子茎で古名は「つくづくし」。春に河原の土手や線路沿い、庭などにも顔を出すので都会人にも身近な野草だろう。正岡子規の随筆にも、妹が赤羽の土手で土筆摘みをしてくる話が見える。茹でてお浸し、玉子とじなどにするが、開いた胞子嚢といわゆる袴を取ると存外小さくなってしまうので、味わうにはかなりの本数が必要である。

This is a reddish light brown, similar to *umezome iro* (the color of a dye created with tree bark and roots of plum). *Tsukushi* (*tsuku-zukushi* in ancient Japanese) is the spore-bearing stem of field horsetail. *Tsukushi* is familiar to most Japanese, even city-dwellers, and can be found on riverbanks, along railways, and in home gardens in the springtime. In a memorable essay, *Shiki Masaoka* wrote about his sister picking field horsetails on the riverbank in *Akabane*. *Tsukushi* is edible boiled, or is cooked with eggs. As these plants become very tiny when the spore cases and gnarl are removed, a fairly large amount is needed to make a savory dish.

土筆色

Tsukushi-iro

つくし

猩猩袴色

Shojo-bakama iro

しょうじょうばかま

赤みがかった薄紫。山葡萄の実の色、古代の葡萄（えび）色を浅くした色ともいえる。猩猩袴は山の斜面や湿地に生えるユリ科の多年草で、早春に花茎を伸ばして六弁の紅紫色の花を総状に咲かせる。「猩猩」は中国の伝説上の霊獣（一説にはオランウータン）で、その赤い毛色のイメージから動植物の名前に冠してよく用いられる。花の色から猩猩を、葉が広がり垂れるところから袴の形にたとえられ、名づけられた。

This is a reddish light purple, the color of native grapes–lighter than the ancient *ebi iro*. *Shojo-bakama* is a perennial liliaceae herb grown on mountain slopes or in damp ground. In early spring, this plant bears six-petaled reddish-purple flowers on raceme stalks. The word "*shojo*" is often used as a prefix for the names of reddish animals and plants, as "*shojo*" originally referred to a legendary Chinese animal (some argue this animal was in fact the orangutan). "*Bakama*" (or "*hakama*") is named for its radiating pattern of leaves, resembling a Japanese ceremonial skirt (*hakama*).

董色

Sumire iro

すみれ

明るい紫。英語色名も同じくバイオレット（スミレ）。紫草の根、紫根を染料にして紫より気持ち青く染め上げる。日本は約70種の董が自生する世界でも有数の生育地域で、万葉の昔から歌に詠まれてきた身近な春の花といえる。パンジーなどの西洋種にくらべ日本の董は小さく楚々としていて、芭蕉も句に詠んだように「何やらゆかし」おもむきがある。ちなみに董の語源は花の形が「墨入れ（墨壺）」に似ているからとも、摘み花にする「ツミレ」からとも。

Violet, or light purple. This color has a hint of blue, dyed with *shikon*, or gromwell root. Japan is one of the largest habitats for violets, with some 70 native varieties. This spring flower is thus quite familiar to the Japanese, dating back to the period of the Anthology of Ten Thousand Leaves. Japanese violets are smaller and more discreet than western pansies, with a subtle appeal, as recounted in a celebrated *haiku* poem by *Basho*. The word "*sumire*" is said to derive from "*sumi-ire*" (ink bottle) for its shape, or perhaps from "*tsumire*" (literally, "picking flowers").

辛夷色

Kobushi-iro

こぶし

灰がかった薄い赤みの白。薄い灰桜と
もいえる。辛夷はモクレン科の落葉高
木で、春に木蓮よりやや早く、葉に先立
って香り高い大形の白い花を咲かせ
る。白い花はその基部でわずかに紅
色を帯び、その色合を色名とする。蕾
を薬用にしたり樹皮から油を採るほ
か、材は緻密で器具や建築に用いられ
るなど昔から人間との関わりの深い樹
木といえる。また、里山で田打ちや里
芋の植え付けの時期を知らせてくれる
春の木でもあった。

A grayish-white tinted with red, or a
light grayish *sakura* (cherry flower).
The *kobushi* is a deciduous
magnoliaceous tree. This plant bears
large, aromatic white flowers before its
leaves bud in the spring, just before the
magnolia bloom. The flowers are
slightly red at the bottom of the petal,
and it is this tint of red that gives this
color its name. This tree is very useful;
the buds of its flowers are used in
medicine, oil can be extracted from its
bark, and its hard wood has been used
in architecture and in the making of
various tools and instruments. This
springtime bloom signals to the farmer
that it is time to plow the rice fields and
to plant Japanese taros.

35

雪柳色

Yukiyanagi iro

ゆきやなぎ

薄い灰白色。ほぼ白鼠（しろねずみ）と
同色といってもいい。雪柳はバラ科の
落葉低木。もともと川岸の岩場などに自
生するが広く庭木として植えられてい
る。春、桜と同じころに、緑の若葉が出
ると同時に白い小さな花を枝一面に咲
かし、雪が積もったような美しさを見せ
てくれる。細かな白い花を米粒に譬え
て、別名コゴメバナ、コゴメザクラとも。

This is a light-grayish white, almost the
same color as *shiro-nezumi iro*.
Yukiyanagi is a deciduous rosaceous
shrub that grows naturally on rocky
riverbanks; the plant is also commonly
found in home gardens. In spring, at the
same time as the cherry blossoms, small
white flowers bloom like a dense
covering of snow over the young green
leaves. This plant is also called
"*kogome-bana*" (literally, "small rice
flowers") or "*kogome-zakura*" ("small
rice cherry flowers"), comparing its tiny
flowers to grains of rice.

41

雛祭り
Hina-matsuri (the Doll's Festival)

古代中国では三月最初の巳（み）の日に禊（みそぎ）をして邪気を祓う習慣があり、これを上巳（じょうし）の節句とよぶ。これが日本に伝わり、次第に三月三日に固定され、川辺に出て宴を開き（曲水の宴）祓え（はらえ）を行う宮中行事となった。その後、人形（ひとがた）に穢れや病を託して川へ流す行事と結びつき、現在も残る「流し雛」の行事、雛祭りの源流となる。一方、平安時代から女の子の人形遊びはあり、これを雛遊び（雛は「ひひな」で小さな玩具の人形のこと）と呼んだ。十六世紀末、この雛遊びが節句行事と一緒になって、女児の節句としての雛祭りが誕生したらしい。江戸初期には簡素な紙雛だったものも、やがて豪華な内裏雛、随身官女（ずいしんかんじょ）、調度の段飾りが登場し、現在に至る。雛人形は母方の里が贈り、嫁入りに持参していくのが習わしとされていた。

In ancient China, people would perform ablutions on the day of the snake in the third month of the Chinese calendar; this seasonal event was called *joshi-no-sekku*. This custom was imported to Japan and became a royal event. On the third day of the third month of the lunar calendar, nobles used to have feasts (called *kyoku-sui no en*) to ward off evil spirits on the riverbanks. Later, people began a tradition of throwing dolls into the river, a ritual believed to carry away impurities and sickness. This custom came to be called *nagashi-bina*, and is the origin of the Doll's Festival. On the other hand, dolls have been the most popular toys among girls since the Heian period, and the phrase *hina-asobi* was coined to mean "playing with dolls." At the end of sixteenth century, *hina-asobi* and the seasonal festival in the third month were reportedly combined to become the Doll's Festival. In the early Edo period, *hina* dolls were very simple and made from paper. Over time, people started to display elaborate dolls of the emperor and empress, along with attendants and luxurious miniature furniture. It was a tradition for the mother's family to send *hina* dolls to granddaughters, with the girls including these dolls among their trousseaus.

梅は、奈良時代以前に中国から渡来した植物で、漢才の趣が強かった奈良や平安時代では、春を告げる花として日本古来の桜にも増して愛されてきた。寒中に他の花に先駆けて咲く凛々しい姿と芳香が、春の訪れを予祝するものとして貴ばれ、その気位と品性が愛でられた。誰もがよく知る梅鉢紋は、梅の五弁花を簡略化した形であり、六つの円で表した六曜を象って吉祥紋としている。

Japanese plum was introduced from China before the Nara period. Its flowers have long been loved by the Japanese, for ages even more popular than cherry blossoms as a sign of spring: elegant plum flowers blooming in the still-cold weather, their scent heralding the coming of spring. The famous family crest, *umebachi-mon*, derived from a five-petaled plum flower, has long been considered an auspicious symbol.

梅文様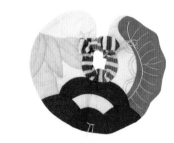

Japanese plum pattern

うめ

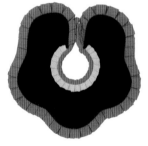

桃文様

Peach pattern

もも

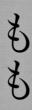

桃は、『古事記』で伊弉諾（いざなぎ）が黄泉の鬼神を避ける実として用いたことが記されるように、邪気を祓う霊木とされた。また、中国の神仙伝説に現れる不老不死の仙女・西王母が住む園には、実を結ぶのに六千年もかかるという桃の木があり、この実を食べれば太陽や月の寿命ほどに長寿が得られるという伝説があった。「桃栗三年　柿八年」の言葉も、このように物事の成就に時間が必要なことを表している。

Long ago, the peach tree was considered a spiritual tree, capable of warding off evil. In the Record of Ancient Matters, *Izanagi,* finding himself in the realm of the dead, drives demons away with peaches. The Chinese legend of *Seioubo* mentions a peach tree that takes six years to bear its fruits, which bestow immortality when eaten. Peaches have been often used metaphorically to describe things that require many years to come to fruition.

牡丹が我が国に伝わったのは奈良時代。その豪奢な華やかさから「花の王」とされ、平安時代には藤原氏筆頭の近衛家の専用文様に使われたり、女性達の華麗な衣装の文様や色に広く利用された。文様にも、豪華な花姿から富貴の象徴として描かれ、壮子が夢の中で蝶に化して牡丹と戯れる逸話を取り上げた「牡丹に蝶」が、また能や謡曲の「石橋（しゃっきょう）」に因んで、文殊菩薩の眷属（けんぞく）の獅子が法華経を賛じて牡丹花と戯れる姿の「獅子に牡丹」が描かれる。

The tree peony was imported from China in the Nara period. Known as the "king of flowers" due to its luxurious appearance, in the Heian period it was depicted in the exclusive crest of the noble *Konoe* family, and later used widely–to stunning effect–in women's kimono patterns. The tree peony has thus come to stand as a symbol of nobility and wealth. The flower is also used as a motif in Japanese-style paintings, such as "Tree Peonies and Butterflies" and "Lions and Tree Peonies," works of art based on traditional stories.

牡丹文様

Tree peony pattern

ぼたん

端午の節句

「端午（五）」は月初めの五日の意味だが、特に五月五日をさすようになった。この日に菖蒲や蓬を飾って邪気を祓い、延命長寿を願う習慣は中国が源流だが、日本にも古代に伝わり宮中行事となった。また、この日には競馬、騎射などの競技を行うので男子の節句とされた。平安後期以降、宮中行事としては廃れたが、鎌倉・室町時代になり、男子の節句、「尚武（武をたっとぶ）」に通ずる「菖蒲」の節句として、武家のあいだで盛んに祝われるようになり、江戸幕府では大名、旗本の登城する式日とされ祝いの柏餅が下賜された。武家では伝来の甲冑を飾り、旗指物を立てたが、庶民のあいだでは疫病神を追い払う神である鍾馗（しょうき）や武者絵の幟（のぼり）を立てたり作り物の甲冑を飾るようになる。男児の健康や出世を願う鯉幟の登場は江戸時代も後半のことである。粽（ちまき）、菖蒲湯、菖蒲酒など邪気祓いの意味合いは現在でも色濃く残っている。

The word *tango* originally meant the fifth day of the month, but it specifically came to connote the fifth day of the fifth month of the lunar calendar. The custom of displaying irises and tansy flowers to ward off evil sprits and to hope for a long life came from China to become a royal event in Japan. This day grew into a boys' festival from the outdoor events such as horse racing and equestrian archery contests that were held on this date. After the late Heian period, these events were no longer observed in the Imperial court. Instead, in the Kamakura and Muromachi periods, *samurai* families began to celebrate what was known as the Iris Festival; indeed, the word *shobu* means both "iris" and "prowess in a martial art." The government of Edo served *kashiwa-mochi* (a rice cake wrapped in an oak leaf) on this ceremonial day, when feudal lords would visit the Edo castle. While *samurai* families displayed ancestral armor and banners, ordinary people would adorn their houses with fake armor and banners bearing the image of the Chinese god *Shoki*, or with a samurai image. In the late Edo period people began to display carp streamers in the hopes of securing a boy's good health and future success. Symbols such as a *chimaki* (a rice cake), a *shobu* herbal bath, and *shobu* herbal sake to ward off evil remain prevalent in connection with this festival.

男児の着物

Boy's Kimono

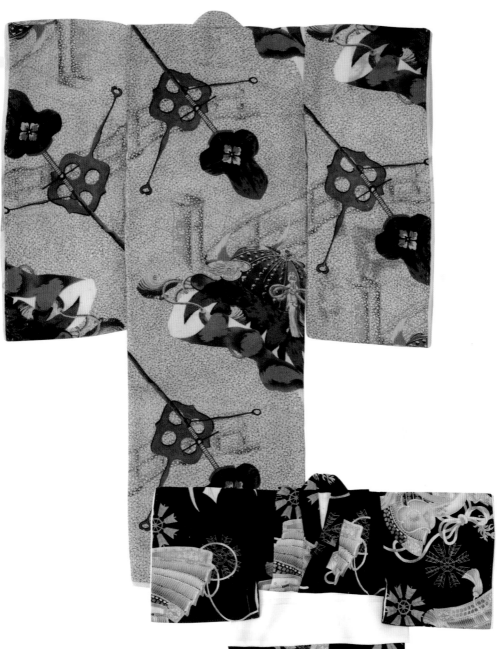

初夏、梅雨、盛夏——四季の移り変わりのなかでも夏はさまざまな表情を見せる。植物たちもその時々の色合を見せてくれる。初夏の青空のもと新緑が薫り、花々はあざやかな色を主張する。梅雨に濡れる花々は楚々としてしとやかだ。照りつける日射しの下、赤、橙色の花は太陽に対峙する。変化と躍動感が夏の色だといってよい。

Early summer, the rainy season, midsummer...the season has many different faces. Summer plants can vary depending on the varying weather. In the early summer, fresh green leaves contrast strikingly against the blue sky as bright flowers stand out against the background, while flowers drenched with dew take on more discreet tones in the rainy season. At the height of summer, splendorous red or orange flowers match the blazing sun. The colors of summer are various and vibrant.

夏

summer

あざやかな青みを帯びた紫。菖蒲（し
ょうぶ／あやめ）色と同色とされる。紫
根と椿灰の灰汁を用いて染めたが、古
代にはカキツケバナといって杜若の花
の汁を用いて摺染をしたといわれる。
杜若はアヤメ科の多年草で湿地に育
ち、幅広い剣状の葉を立て、5〜6月に
美しい濃紫の花を咲かせる。同属のア
ヤメ、ハナショウブより古くから日本人
に愛されてきた花である。杜若という
漢字名は中国ではヤブミョウガなど別
種の植物名。「燕子花」の字もあてる。

杜若色

Kakitsubata iro

かきつばた

This is a bright bluish purple, the same
color as *ayame/shobu iro* (the color of
irises). This color is generally dyed with
lye from camellia ash, but in ancient
times, the flower juice of *kakitsubata*
seems to have been used in the *suri
zome* dyeing technique. *Kakitsubata* is
a perennial iridaceous plant that grows
in damp fields, with wide sword-like
leaves and beautiful, thick purple
flowers that bloom in May and June.
This plant has been long cherished by
the Japanese, even before congeneric
plants such as *ayame* and *hana-shobu*
became popular. Interestingly, the
Chinese characters used in Japan to
indicate *kakitsubata* have a different
meaning in China, referring to a
different kind of plant (*yabu-myoga*).

麦藁色

Mugiwara-iro

むぎわら

やや青みを帯びた淡黄色。麦の穂を
刈り取った後の茎の色。初夏、麦の収
穫を迎える季節を麦秋とよび、その頃
から加工されて出回るまだ青みの残る
新麦藁は盛夏へ向けての好もしい風物
だった。ストローの麦藁、麦藁細工の
小箱、麦藁帽子などが懐かしい。

This is the color of straw, but with a tint
of blue. In early summer, the time of
the wheat harvest is called *"bakushu"*
or *"mugiaki"* (literally, "wheat
autumn"); products of still-fresh straw
that come available in this season—
straw hats and boxes, for example—are
nostalgic symbols of the start of
midsummer.

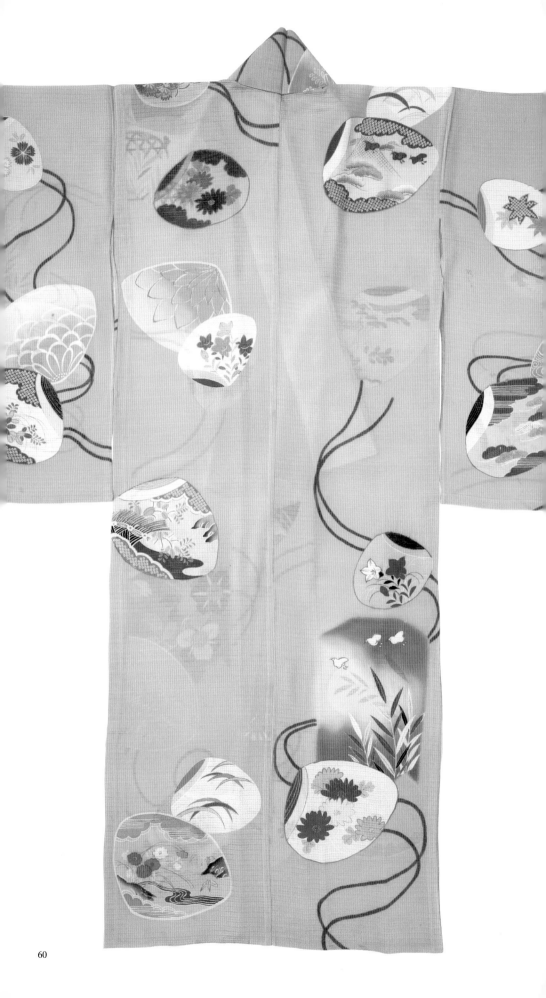

忘れ草色

Wasuregusa iro

わすれぐさ

明るい黄赤。蜜柑（みかん）色とほぼ同色。忘れ草はユリ科の植物ヤブカンゾウ、ノカンゾウの別名で、原野の溝のへりや土手に多く自生する。盛夏に50〜80cmの茎を直立させて黄赤色のユリに似た花を咲かせる。古来日本人に親しまれてきた花で、忘れ草の名は身につけると物思いを忘れるという言い伝えによる。『万葉集』などでもそのように歌われている。

A bright yellowish-red, almost the same as *mikan* iro (the color of Japanese mandarin). *Wasuregusa* is a nickname for the *yabukanzo* liliaceae plant, (Hemerocallis fulva form. kwanso, or *nokanzo*) common on riverbanks and on the roadside. The stems of this plant extend 50 - 80 cm in height and bear yellowish-red lily-like flowers in midsummer, appealing to the Japanese eye since ancient times. The name *"wasuregusa"* comes from a legend recounted in the Anthology of Ten Thousand Leaves attesting to the plant's soothing qualities.

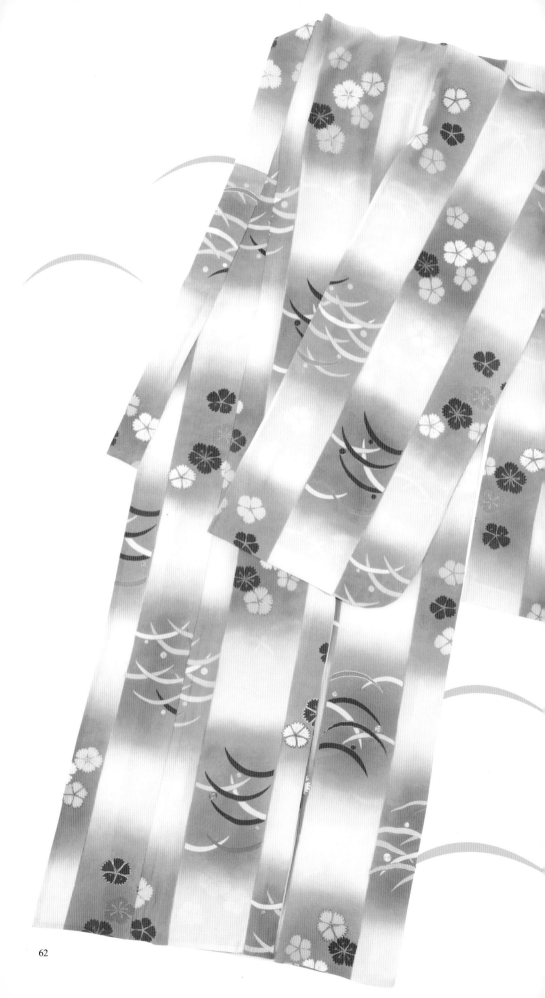

石竹色

Sekichiku iro

せきちく

薄い赤紫。発色によっては黄を帯びる。石竹はナデシコ科の多年草で、平安時代に中国から伝わり、日本に自生していた河原撫子（大和撫子）に対して「唐撫子」とも呼ばれる。5〜7月、白・赤・紫の鋭く切れ込んだ五弁花を咲かせ、四季咲きの品種があることから「常夏」とも呼ばれる。古来、撫子は着物などの図案に用いられてきたが、石竹の普及によって江戸時代ではこちらのほうが多く描かれるようになる。

This is a light red-purple, sometimes yellowish, depending on the way the dye takes to the fabric. *Sekichiku* is a perennial caryophyllaceous plant imported from China in the Heian period. This plant is also called "*kara-nadeshiko*" (Chinese pink or dianthus chinensis), in contrast to "*kawara-nadeshiko*" or "*yamato nadeshiko*" (native Japanese pink). *Sekichiku* bears five-petaled, serrated-edged flowers in white, red, and purple from May to July. The perennial variety of this plant is nicknamed "*tokonatsu*" (everlasting summer). *Nadeshiko* has long been used in kimono designs, while *sekichiku* became more popular after the Edo period.

檜扇色

Hiougi iro

ひおうぎ

濃い黄赤。ほぼ緋（ひ）色といってよい。檜扇はアヤメ科の多年草で、夏に赤い斑点をもつ黄赤色の花を咲かせる。もともと檜扇は、宮中で衣冠・直衣姿の際、笏にかえて用いた檜の薄板を重ねた扇のことで、花の形が似ているために名づけられた。檜扇の花にもまして知られる黒々とした種子は、射干玉（ぬばたま）と呼ばれ、その黒さから『万葉集』以来「ぬばたま」は黒、夜に掛かる枕詞とされてきた。

This is a thick yellow-red, almost the same color as scarlet. *Hiougi* is a blackberry lily, a perennial iridaceous plant that yields yellow-red flowers with tiny red dots in the summer. *Hiougi* originally referred to cypress fans, formerly standard accessories with everyday kimono in the Imperial court (as opposed to the mace, the standard accessory with ceremonial kimono). The word came to refer to this plant due to the fan-like shape of its flowers. The raven-black seeds of *hiougi* are even more famous, widely known as "*nubatama*." This word has been used as a synonym for "black" and "night" since the Anthology of Ten Thousand Leaves.

立葵色

Tachi-aoi iro

たちあおい

やや暗く濃い紅赤色。あざやかな濃紅
色である韓紅（からくれない）をいくぶ
ん沈ませた色合。立葵は草丈2m近く
になるアオイ科の越年草で、夏に白・ピ
ンク・紅の大きな花を下から上に順次
咲き上がらせる。現在、園芸でいう葵
はこの立葵のことである。京都賀茂神
社の葵祭にゆかりの葵はフタバアオイ
のことで、立葵とは別種の植物。

A darkish ruby, slightly darker than
kara-kurenai (bright dark red). *Tachi-
aoi* (hollyhock) is a biennial malvaceous
plant that grows to 2 m and bears large
white, pink, and ruby flowers that
bloom from the bottom of the stalk to
the top in summer. On its own, the
word *aoi* generally connotes its use in
tachi-aoi, although in the context of the
Aoi Matsuri festival at the *Kamo* shrine
in Kyoto, this word is used with
reference to *futaba-aoi* (asarum
caulescens).

夏椿色

Natsu-tsubaki iro

なつつばき

黄みの白。鳥の子紙の色である鳥の子色に近い。夏椿はツバキ科の落葉高木で、滑らかな木肌をもち、6〜7月に椿に似た白い花を咲かせる。山地に自生し、神奈川県の箱根などには見事な林があるが、近年はその姿形が愛され、庭木として多く植えられるようになっている。別名の「沙羅（しゃら）の木」は、釈迦入滅の折に花を咲かせたといわれる沙羅の花に似ているところから。

A yellowish-white, similar to *torinoko-iro* (the color of *torinoko-gani*, a kind of Japanese paper). *Natsu-tsubaki* (Japanese stewartia) is a deciduous theaceous tree with a silky surface bearing camellia-like white flowers in June and July. Growing naturally in mountains and forming beautiful native bushes in Hakone, Kanagawa prefecture, this plant is also very popular as a garden tree. The *natsu-tsubaki* is called a "sal tree," for the shape of its flowers, which resemble the sal flowers said to bloom when the Buddha entered nirvana.

露草色

Tsuyukusa iro

つゆくさ

あざやかな紫みの青。ラピスラズリの色
である瑠璃（るり）色に近い。古来、実
際の露草（鴨頭草）の花汁を用いた摺
染の露草色があったが、すぐに褪色し
青灰色になってしまうことから、移ろい
やすさの象徴として歌に詠まれてきた。
露草は日本全国に自生する一年草で、
夏から秋、二枚貝状の苞（ほう）の間か
ら蝶の形の花を咲かせる。友禅染や絞
り染の下絵に用いる青花紙は、この露
草の花の絞り汁を染み込ませたもの。

A bright purplish blue, the color of
lapis lazuli. *Tsuyukusa-iro* was used in
poetry as a metaphor for transience,
because in ancient times this color used
to be created with *tsuyukusa* dye (made
from Asian day flowers) and easily
changed to a grayish blue. *Tsuyukusa* is
a native annual herb common
throughout Japan, with butterfly-
shaped flowers stemming from clam-
like bracts from summer to autumn.
This flower is also used for *aobanagami*
(paper stained with blue pigment
extracted from dayflowers) used in
rough sketches for *Yuzen* dyeing and
tie-dyeing.

額紫陽花色

Gaku-ajisai iro

がくあじさい

薄い紫。藍と呉藍（紅花）で染めた薄
二藍（うすふたあい）に近い色。額紫陽
花はユキノシタ科の落葉低木。梅雨の
頃、中心部に両性花を密生させ周縁に
萼片だけが発達した中性花を咲かせ
る。この萼の花色。日本原産で、中性
花だけを毬のように咲かせる普通の紫
陽花は、額紫陽花を改良したものとさ
れている。大玉のようになる紫陽花に
くらべ楚々とした姿が美しい。

This is a light purple, similar to usu-
futa-ai, the color of a dye created with
indigo and safflower. Gaku-ajisai
(lacecup hydrangea) is a deciduous
saxifragaceous shrub, bearing thick
clusters of bisexual flowers in the center
and neutral flowers with petal-like
calyxes on the edge. This color
corresponds to the color of this calyx.
This plant is a native of Japan, from
which it is assumed ordinary hydrangea
was bred for ornamental use.
Gakuajisai has a humble beauty
compared the large balls of flowers
abloom on the ordinary hydrangea.

牽牛織女の星合い伝説は古い時代に中国から日本に伝わったもので『万葉集』などにも多く歌われている。織女を日本風にいうと「棚機女（たなばたつめ）」、これが「たなばた」の語源で、後に七月七日の夕の字をあてた。伝説とともにその日の行事「乞巧奠（きこうでん）」も伝わり、織女星に裁縫、書道などの技芸の上達を願い、庭に供物を並べるという宮中、貴族の行事となったが、ここにはお馴染みの笹竹の七夕飾りはまだ姿を見せない。一方、民間では古くから七月十五日の盂蘭盆の前行事として人形などの形代（かたしろ）流しの禊、また精霊の依り代として笹竹を立てる行事があった。さらに七夕の夜には必ず雨が降るという伝承から水神祭りとの関りさえも窺え、こうした複雑に混じり合った民間信仰と乞巧奠（きこうでん）の行事が重なり、笹竹に願い事の短冊を吊るす七夕行事が生まれたといわれている。

The legend of Altair and Vega was imported from China to ancient Japan and is referred to often throughout the Anthology of Ten Thousand Leaves. Vega is associated with a legendary Japanese weaver named *Tanabata-tsume*. The name of the festival is said to come from her name. The kanji characters indicating tanabata mean "the evening of the seventh." Another Chinese legend, *Kikouden*, was also imported along with the legend of Altair and Vega, and these legends were transformed into an Imperial event in which nobles presented offerings to Vega in a garden, hoping for progress in artistic skills such as sewing and calligraphy. Among the general population, dolls were thrown into the river to ward off evil on the seventh day of the seventh month in the lunar calendar as a ceremony in preparation for the *Urabon* festival on the fifteenth day of the seventh month. Also on the seventh day of the seventh month, people would hang bamboo grass to serve as perches for the ancestral spirits. This festival is also associated with the separate festival of the god of water, because it often rains on the evening of *tanabata*. The combination of these associated folk beliefs and the Chinese custom of *Kikouden* led to an ongoing tradition in which people write their wishes on strips of colorful paper and hang them from bamboo branches.

菖蒲（あやめ）、杜若、花菖蒲は混同されることが多い。菖蒲（あやめ）は乾燥地に生え、杜若と花菖蒲は湿地に咲く。また花が咲くのもこの順序である。宮中では五月五日の端午の節句に香袋に菖蒲を添えて薬玉をつくり、これを柱や御簾にかけて邪気を払う風習があった。しかし、この時に用いた本来の菖蒲は葉の形こそ菖蒲（あやめ）に似るが、強い芳香を持った別種の植物であり、「菖蒲湯」などにはこちらが使われた。また、川に渡す板橋と杜若の「八橋の図」は『伊勢物語』に因んだ文様で、在原業平の歌芸と美貌にあやかろうと子供の衣装に表したのか。

Kakitsubata, hana-shobu, and *ayame* are three different irises often confused with one another. *Ayame* grows in dry ground, while *kakitsubata* and *hana-shobu* grow in marshy areas. *Ayame* blooms first, followed by *kakitsubata* and then *hana-shobu.* In the Imperial court on Boy's Day, *shobu* were placed in a sachet and hung on columns and bamboo blinds to ward off evil spirits. The leaves of *shobu* and *ayame* look much alike but *shobu* has a stronger scent and was used for *shobu-yu* (a *shobu* herbal bath). The pattern of *yatsuhashi-no-zu* (an eight-plank bridge with irises) based on the Tales of Ise was depicted on children's kimono, perhaps because people hope that their children will follow the example of *Ariwara-no-Narihira*, both in his beauty and in his poetic talents.

菖蒲文様

Ayame pattern

あやめ

貝と一緒によく描かれるのが海松。海底の貝は神仙境の竜宮に住む生物と考えられ、宝物の一つとされる。海藻の海松は、松枝のように海中で揺らぐ房々とした茎を「みるふさ」と呼んで美しい女性の髪に例えた。さらに、珊瑚は古くから七宝の一つとされ、女性を飾る宝飾品として用いられてきた。こうしたことから、貝のように貞節で、見目が麗しく美しい髪姿の禍福な人生を送りたいと願って、貝と海藻の文様が女性の衣服や婚礼道具に飾られたのである。一方、堅固な貝殻を強い護りに例えて、武士が甲斐ある人生などと洒落て見たのも貝文様である。

Miru (sea moss) is often depicted in combination with seashells. Shelled creatures were treasured because they were believed to live in the Dragon Palace in *Shinsenkyo*, an immortal undersea paradise. *Miru* has long been appreciated for its sleek, wavy appearance. *Miru*'s thick stems were called *mirufusa*, and were often used as a metaphor for a woman's luxuriant hair. Corals, also depicted in this pattern, were deemed one of the celebrated "seven treasures" and were often used in women's accessories. The pattern of seashells and sea moss often adorned women's kimonos and trousseaus to symbolize virtue, beauty, and life's richness. Seashells were also the symbol of a strong defense and the virtues of the samurai life.

貝と海松文様

Seashells and
sea moss pattern

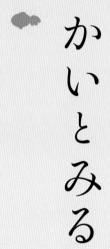

かいとみる

風鈴文様

Wind bells pattern

ふうりん

そよ風に吹かれて爽やかに鳴る風鈴。そんな風鈴が蒸し暑い日本の盛夏に涼味を添える。如何にも日本情趣を満喫させる風物のようだが、風鈴も元は中国から伝わったもので最初は貝殻や金属で作られていた。ビードロ製の風鈴が登場したのは江戸時代後期のことで、「江戸風鈴」と呼ばれていた。忙しく鳴く蝉の声にかき消されるように、チリリンチリリンと鳴らしながら売り声も掛けずに売り歩いた風鈴売りの姿が夏の風物詩だった。貝合せ、扇、梅、蜻蛉、笹などの夏の風情を絵風鈴に描き、今も江戸の下町に伝え残る風物である。

Furin, or wind chimes, add a refreshing note to a humid midsummer moment in Japan. These chimes look quintessentially Japanese but in fact were originally imported from China. In the early days, they were made of shells and metal. Painted-glass wind chimes appeared in the latter half of the Edo period and therefore are also called *Edo furin.* Vendors carrying a number of wind chimes on a pole, harmonizing to the buzzing of cicadas, were a typical summer feature. Wind chimes featuring pictures of *kaiawase,* fans, plums, green drakes, or bamboo grasses remain traditional sights of summer in older areas of Tokyo.

波文様

Wave pattern

なみ

古くは、波や魚の文様は遥か東海にある蓬莱の島に続く広い海原を表す文様とされてきた。波は果てることなく永遠の彼方に広がる、また押し寄せて引いて滞ることのない海の胎動を表し、永遠と不滅、彼岸、長寿などを意味して吉祥の最たる文様とされている。川の流水や湧き出る泉の渦紋も同様に考えられている。勢いよく怒濤と押し寄せて、厳に砕け散る波は「男波」と称され、何にも挫けず引くことのない証しとし、またよく知られる「青海波」は舞楽に用いられた衣服から発した文様であり、大陸にある内陸の湖の静かな波を表しているといわれる。

Long ago, the pattern of waves and fish represented the vast oceans that led to the immortal *Horai* island. A wave pattern is considered to be among the most auspicious of designs in its expression of the coming and going of the tide, or perpetual movement of the sea, which is in itself a metaphor for eternity and immortality, the equinoctial week, and a long life. Swirling patterns, representing river streams and spring water, are also considered auspicious. Raging wild waves are called *otoko-nami* (literally, "male waves"), representing an unbreakable spirit, while the famous *seigaiha* pattern, derived from costumes for court dances and music, is said to represent the quiet waves of an inland lake.

王朝時代、宮中に献上する「虫狩り」が嵯峨野で行われたり、虫の姿や鳴き声を競う「虫競べ」のために、貴族の屋敷で虫が飼われたりした。また、『源氏物語』の二十八帖で、野分（台風）が吹き荒れた翌朝、源氏の文を携えた夕霧が六条院邸を訪れると、そこには女の童が庭に降りて草の玉露を集めて虫に与える光景があった。それを垣間見た夕霧はいとも美しく好ましく思えたのである。こんな、雅な王朝風景を表して夏草や秋草と虫籠文様がよく描かれる。昔から、空中に飛び去って見えなくなってしまう虫は、来世に魂を運ぶ生き物として考えられてきた。

In the Heian period, the nobles went insect hunting in *Sagano*, Kyoto to make gifts of these insects to the court; these hunters would also keep insects in their houses for contests based on appearance and the insects' particular sounds. In chapter 28 of the Tale of Genji, when *Yugiri* delivers a letter from *Genji* to the *Rokujoin* House the morning after a typhoon, he is charmed by the beauty of a little girl giving dewdrops to garden insects. Insect cages are drawn along with summer or autumn plants, in homage to the graceful Imperial court. Because insects fly away and disappear into the sky, they were long ago seen as creatures that deliver souls to the afterlife.

虫籠文様

Insect cage pattern

むしかご

浴衣

Yukata (summer kimono)

浴後または夏に着る木綿の単（ひとえ）
の着物。古くは麻製で湯帷子（かたび
ら）と称して入浴時にこれを着て湯に
入った。そのため、湯帷子が転じて浴
衣の名が生まれた。後に木綿製となり
湯上がりの身拭い用や、浴後の衣料と
なっていく。元は袖口下を縫いふさが
ない広袖仕立てだったが、盆踊りなど
の衣装、雨具、道中の塵よけ、労働着
や夏の家庭内での日常着として着られ
るようにもなる。第二次大戦後、子ども
の浴衣は盛夏の外出着として用途が拡
大され、振袖や可愛い袖がつけられて
楽しいものとなった。

Yukata is a cotton kimono wore after
bathing or in summer. Long ago, as it
was made from hemp and used as
bathing kimono, this garment was
called a *yukatabira* (meaning "hot bath
single kimono"), the origin of the name
yukata. Later, the *yukata* came to be
made of cotton and used as a kimono
to wear after bathing. Sleeves were
wider in olden times. *Yukata* came to
have a range of uses: as a costume for
the Bon festival, on some occasions as
raincoats or smocks, as popular home
wear in the summer, and as work
clothes. After WW II, children's *yukata*
came to be used as streetwear in
midsummer, adorned with beautiful
sleeves in various lengths.

93

法被・半纏

法被は下級武士や中間（ちゅうげん）などが江戸時代に用いた上着で、羽織に似た広袖で胸紐がついたものをさす。また半纏は庶民の略装で、袷や綿入れにして寒さを防いだ上着である。形は法被に似るが、袖を細く筒袖にする。特に職人が着た印半纏は木綿製で紺地に文字や標目を白で染め抜き、法被と混同することが多い。共に近代では祭りに用いられ、法被は絹の模様物を使って囃子方（はやしかた）や踊り手が着用し、印半纏は山車方（だしかた）が着用することが多い。子どもらもそれに従い、法被と印半纏を着て祭りに参加した。

Happi is an outer coat with wide sleeves and strips of cloth in front, and was worn by lower-ranking samurai in the Edo period. On the other hand, *hanten* is a two-ply or padded jacket worn by ordinary citizens. The hanten's sleeves are thinner and cylindrical, but otherwise *happi* and *hanten* are similar garments. In particular, craftsmen's *hanten*, which were called *shirushi-banten*, were confused with *happi* because both were made from cotton and dyed dark blue, with patterns or writing depicted with resist. In modern times, *happi* and *hanten* are both worn in traditional festivals; silk *happi* with patterns are worn by musicians and dancers, while *shirushi-banten* are worn by teams pulling parade floats. Children also wear *happi* or *hanten* to join the festivals.

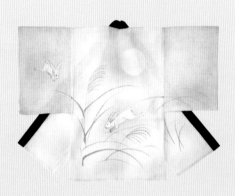

秋は実りの季節。色の主役は、花から
果実へ、そしてまもなく散り落ちる葉へ
と移る。たわわになった木の実草の実
は艶ある色彩で生命を次代へ繋ぐ。
山々、街路を錦繍に染める紅葉黄葉は
まもなくやってくる眠りの季節を伝える。
そして、寂しげな秋草の花の色合は古
来、日本人があわれに心惹かれてきた
ものといえる。

The season of the harvest changes in
symbolic hues: the colors of flowers,
the colors of fruits, followed by the
colors of the falling leaves. Abundant,
shiny fruits pass their seeds to the next
generation. Brilliant autumn leaves
dusting the mountains and carpeting
the streets herald the hibernating
season. The Japanese have long
appreciated the melancholy mood of
autumnal plants.

高雄楓色

Takao-kaede iro

たかおかえで

あざやかな黄みの赤。いわゆる紅葉色よりやや明るく、緋（ひ）色に近い。高雄は京都市西北部、清滝川沿いの紅葉の名所で、神護寺、高山寺などの名刹でも知られる。楓の仲間は日本の山野に30種ほどが自生し、イロハカエデが代表種。その名所高雄にちなんで高雄楓とも呼ばれる。楓のあざやかな紅葉には適度な湿潤、日照、大きな気温差が必要条件で、とくに山地の谷間が名所となることが多い。

This is a brilliant yellowish-red, slightly brighter than maple red, closer to scarlet. Takao, the area along *Kiyotaki* river in northwest of Kyoto, is famous for its autumnal leaves and the beautiful grounds of the *Jingoji* and *Kouzanji* temples. Some 30 varieties of maple trees grow naturally in Japan, most notably the Japanese maple (*acer palmatum*), nicknamed *Takao-kaede* after this area. The best spots for viewing autumnal leaves are generally in mountain areas, where the precise amount of humidity and sunlight, as well as the requisite significant temperature differentials, create the perfect conditions for changing maple foliage.

秋桜色

Kosumosu-iro

こすもす

薄い紫みの赤。英語色名ローズピンクとほぼ同じ。また日本の伝統色である青みの薄赤の紅梅色にも近い。コスモスは明治時代に伝わったメキシコ原産の植物だが、日本の風土によく馴染み、庭植えされるほか広く野生化している。秋に白・ピンク・紅色の花を咲かせる。丈高くなるが全体にやわらかみを帯び、風に揺れる姿が日本人の感性に訴えるものがある。「秋桜」の字をあてたのもその表れといえるだろう。

This is a light purplish red, almost the same hue as rose pink, and closely resembles the traditional Japanese color of *kobai iro* (light pink with a hint of blue). Cosmos is a native of Mexico imported to Japan in the Meiji period. Since then, this plant has adapted well to the Japanese climate, growing widely in the wild and frequently seen in home gardens. In autumn, cosmos bears white, pink, and ruby flowers. The stems are tall but soft, swaying gracefully in the wind, causing appreciative Japanese to refer to these flowers as *"akizakura"* (autumnal cherry blossoms).

櫨色

Hazenoki iro

はぜのき

暗い黄みの赤。伝統色に同じ字の櫨
（はじ）色があるが、こちらは櫨の芯材
を用いて染めた、くすんだ薄赤黄のこ
と。櫨はウルシ科の落葉高木で山地に
自生、果実から木蝋を採るために栽培
もされる。秋、羽状複葉の葉が楓に先
立って真っ赤に紅葉する。実生の幼木
を林仕立てにした盆栽が愛される。

A dark yellowish-red. The traditional
Japanese color "*haji*" uses the same
Chinese characters as *hazenoki*, but
"*haji*" is a subdued light red-yellow, the
color created with the center layer of
the Japanese wax tree. *Hazenoki* is a
deciduous tree of the sumac family,
growing naturally in mountainous
areas. This tree is also cultivated for the
sumac wax yielded by its fruit. Its
pinnate compound leaves turn red in
autumn, before maples. Bonsai of
young *hazenoki* trees are very popular,
raised from seeds and stylized into a
miniature forests.

103

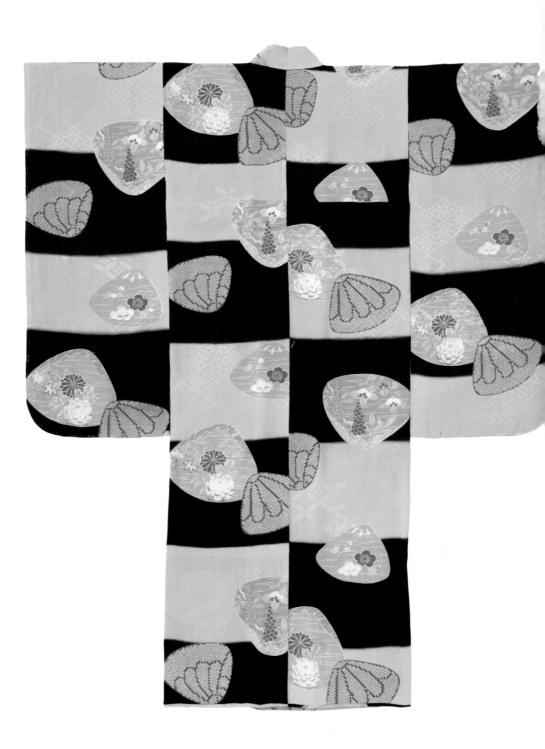

104

の黄。クリームがかった蜜
色ともいえ、枇杷（びわ）の
実の色に似ている。金木犀はモクセイ
科の常緑小高木で庭木によく植えられ
る。9～10月、葉のつけ根に芳香を放
つ橙黄色の小さな花をたくさん咲かせ
る。色名はこの花色から。普段は目立
たない木だが、この季節だけは香りと
こぼれた花片が際立つ。中国では香木
一般を桂と呼び、金木犀の漢名は「丹
桂」。秋の花を代表して「桂秋」という
言葉もある。

A bright reddish-yellow, or the color of
Japanese mandarin tinted with a cream
color, similar to the color of loquat
fruits. *Kinmokusei* (orange osmanthus)
is an evergreen tree in the oleaceous
family, common in home gardens. In
September and October, this plant
bears countless tiny aromatic orange-
yellow flowers where the leaves are
joined. The name of this color derives
from this flower's hue. *Kinmokusei* is a
little-noticed plant–except in the season
when its rich aroma fills the air and its
fallen flowers color the ground. In
China, fragrant woods are collectively
called "*gui*;" orange asmanthus is called
"*dangui*" (literally, "red aroma") or
"*guiqiu*" ("aromatic autumn").

金木犀色

Kinmokusei-iro

きんもくせい

鴨脚色

Icho-iro

いちょう

少しくすんだ緑みの黄色。古代色の深黄（ふかきき）に近い。銀杏色とも書く。鴨脚は中国原産といわれる高さ30mにも達する落葉高木。太古から存在した一科一種の化石のような植物である。古い時代に中国から渡来し、その鳥の水掻きのような葉形を表す「鴨脚（ヤーチャオ）」から日本での名も「いちょう」となった。雌雄異株で雌の木になる実が銀杏（ぎんなん）である。日本各地に街路樹として植えられ、秋を黄金色に彩ってくれる。

A subdued greenish-yellow. This color is similar to the ancient color of *fukaki-ki* (dark yellow). Ginkgo is said to be a native of China, a deciduous tree measuring up to 30 meters in height. This plant is a "living fossil," the sole surviving species of an ancient botanical family, which was imported to Japan from China long ago. The name *"icho"* derives from the Chinese name *"yajiao"* (which means "duck foot"), so named for its web-like leaves. This is a dioecious plant bearing ginkgo nuts on female trees. Ginkgo trees are planted along the streets all over Japan, turning entire cities a golden yellow in autumn.

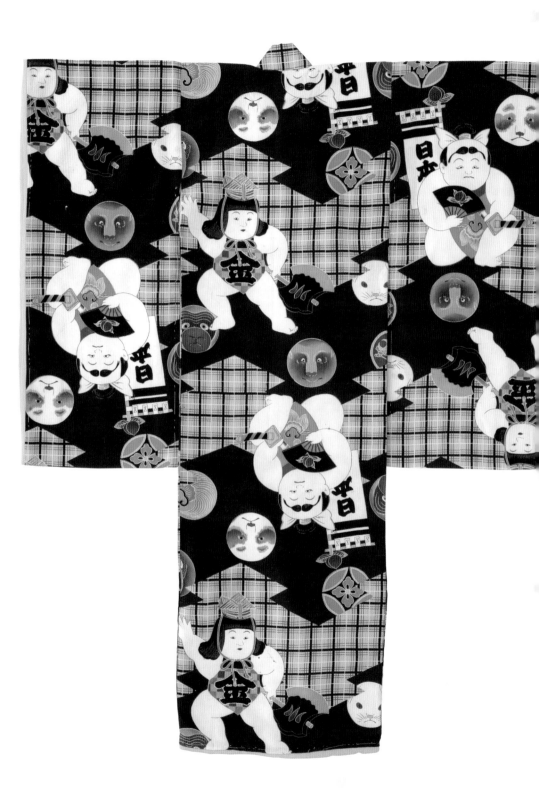

軒忍色

Nokishinobu iro

のきしのぶ

やや暗い濃い緑。いくぶんくすんだ深緑ともいえる。軒忍はウラボシ科のシダ植物で、革質常緑の20cmほどの単葉を生やす。ふつう樹幹や岩石に着生するが、人家の茅葺やこけら葺の屋根の軒に生えることもあってこの名前がついた。『百人一首』順徳院の歌「ももしきや古き軒端のしのぶにも…」でも知られるように、一種うらぶれた風情をもつ植物。京都大原の茶屋などではわざわざ軒に植えている。

A dull or slightly subdued dark green. *Nokishinobu* is a kind of polypod epiphytic fern (polypodiaceae), with leathery leaves approximately 20 centimeters in length. These plants generally grow epiphytically, without harm to the host, on tree trunks, or on rocks, adding a somewhat desolate air to scenery, as recounted in the poem by *Juntoku-In* from "100 Poems By 100 Poets." *Nokishinobu* ferns are planted on the eaves of tea houses in *Ohara*, Kyoto, to create a rustic atmosphere.

団栗色

Donguri iro

どんぐり

明るい茶褐色。焦茶よりやや薄く枯茶よりやや濃い色合。団栗は、椎、樫、栃、櫟（くぬぎ）などブナ科植物の実の総称。「橡栗（とちぐり）」の訛った言葉ともいわれ、その場合は栃、櫟の実を特に指す。ただし櫟の実の色は薄い茶褐色で、その色を表す「橡（つるばみ）色」（黒色を表す橡色とは別名）という伝統色名もある。この団栗色は椎の実、樫の実の色といえるだろう。椎、樫は都会でも公園や古い屋敷の庭に多く、秋、パラパラと道に落ちる音の風情を感じられる。

A light liver color, between *kogecha* (burnt umber) and *karacha* (the brown color of a withered leaf). *Donguri* (acorn) is the collective name for nuts of fagaceae plants, including sawtooth and other oaks and the Japanese horse-chestnut. The nuts of the latter and of the sawtooth oak are sometimes called "*tochiguri,*" through a phonetic transformation from *donguri*. *Donguri-iro* specifically refers to the color of oak acorns, while the traditional name "*tsurubami iro*" refers to the color of sawtooth oak, a lighter brownish-red. Oak trees are commonly found in city parks and in the gardens of older, historical houses in Japan. The sound of falling acorns adds a particular flavor to the autumnal season.

あざやかな紫みの青。桔梗色より気持ち濃いめ。表蘇芳(すおう)、裏青の襲(かさね)の色目でもある。龍胆は山野に自生するリンドウ科の多年草で、笹に似た葉を対生させ、秋、青紫から赤紫の釣鐘形の花を咲かせる。花は日が上ると開き、夜には閉じる。丈は60cmほどにまで伸びるものもあり、秋野に風に揺れて美しい。矮性の園芸種もあり、浅い植木鉢に冠状に葉と花をつける。根は健胃剤の龍胆(りゅうたん)として用いられる。

A stunning purplish blue, slightly darker than *kikyo iro* (the color of Japanese bell-flowers). *Rindo* also refers to the name of a color scheme (including a raspberry red and a blue, for the outer and inner kimono, respectively) in the Heian period. *Rindo* is a perennial gentian plant with distichous bamboo-like leaves that grows naturally on hills, bearing blue-purple or red-purple bell-shaped flowers in autumn. Its flowers bloom in the morning and wilt in the evening. This plant measures up to 60 cm, swaying beautifully in the autumnal breeze. The garden-species dwarf variety is often planted in shallow flower pots. The root of the plant is used in traditional Chinese herbal medicine as a stomachic.

龍胆色

Rindo iro

りんどう

113

紫式部色

Murasaki-shikibu iro

むらさきしきぶ

赤みの紫。紅紫（こうし）色。紫式部は
『源氏物語』の作者名にちなんだ植物
名。クマツヅラ科の落葉低木で、葉の
付け根に咲いた花が秋、5mmほどの
小さな玉のような紫の実を結ぶ。漢名
「紫珠」。葉が落ちた後も実を残し、長
く枝垂れた枝に紫の玉を連ねた姿が
愛される。広く山野に自生するが庭木
としても植えられている。実の小さな小
紫、実の白い白式部もある。

Red purple. *Murasaki-shikibu*
(Japanese beauty berry) is a deciduous
verbenaceous plant, named after the
author of the Tale of Genji. In autumn
this plant bears 5-mm pearl-like purple
berries where the leaves join, referred
to in Chinese as "*zizhu*" (purple
pearls). As these fruits remain even
after the leaves fall off, this plant is
appreciated for its long weeping wands
adorned with purple berries.
Murasaki-shikibu grows naturally on
hills and is also planted in home
gardens. Another plant of this type,
with smaller fruits, is called
"*komurasaki*," and one with white
berries is known as "*shiroshikibu.*"

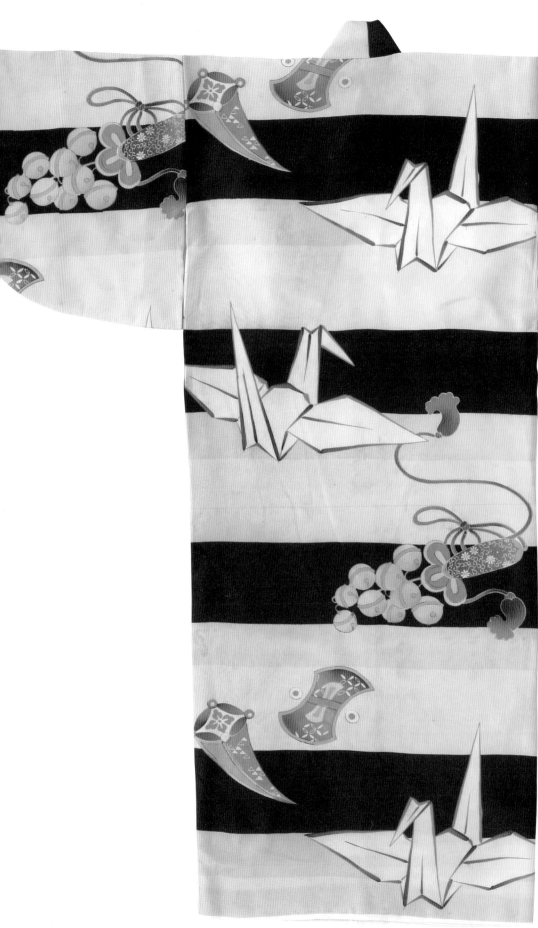

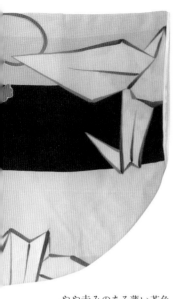

芒色

Susuki iro

すすき

やや赤みのある薄い茶色。丁字（ちょうじ）の樹皮を染料にした丁字色をやや薄くしたような色。芒は日本中に生えているイネ科の多年草で、乾燥した土地を好んでしばしば大群落をつくる。川原などの湿地で大群落をつくっている荻（おぎ）によく似ているため、間違える人も多い。秋、茎の先端に白褐色の花穂をつける。色名はこの穂の色から。この穂を尾花（おばな）と呼び、古来、日本人に親しまれてきた。秋の七草の一つ、十五夜の月見の供え花、茅葺屋根の材料として暮らしに馴染んだ植物である。

A light brown with a hint of red, lighter than *choji iro*, the color of clove bark dye. *Susuki*, or Japanese pampas grass, is a perennial gramineae plant, very common in dry areas all over Japan. This plant is often mistaken for a similar plant, *ogi* (miscanthus sacchariflourus), which grows thickly on riverbanks or in marshes. *Susuki* yields brownish white buds from the top of its stems in autumn. The name of this color is derived from the inflorescence of this plant (which is referred to as *obana*). *Susuki* is one of the seven autumnal flowers and is used as floral tribute in the full-moon ceremony. The plant has also been used traditionally in roofing thatch.

十五夜

Jugoya (Full moon festival)

旧暦八月十五日の「お月見」。この日の中秋の名月を愛でる習慣は古く中国から伝わり、奈良・平安時代に貴族の間に詩歌を詠み、管弦の宴を催す行事として定着していった。一方、旧暦つまり月齢を農作業の目安としていた農村では、昔から満月に収穫を祝い、豊作の祈りを捧げる儀礼の日があった。「芋名月」の名称があるように、稲作伝来以前に東南アジアから伝わった里芋の収穫儀礼があり、それがやがて稲の収穫祭の儀礼にもとりこまれていったものらしい。こんな都の名月観賞と農村での収穫儀礼が結びついて、月を愛で、月に供え物をする十五夜の行事が生まれたといえる。月への供え物は、薄の穂、里芋、月見団子や餅で、また、その供え物を子どもが盗むことを認め、多く盗まれる程にその家の来年の豊作が約束されることがいわれる。八月十五日の「芋名月」に対して、九月十三日を「豆名月」「栗名月」と呼ぶ。

This moon viewing festival takes place on the fifteenth day of the eighth month in the lunar calendar, an event imported from China to ancient Japan. In the Nara and Heian periods, this festival spread among the Japanese aristocracy and became a common event, which the nobles would celebrate by writing poems and throwing parties with music. Meanwhile, people in agricultural villages farmed according to a lunar calendar; their evening full-moon ceremony celebrated the harvest and expressed hopes for an abundant crop. The phrase *imo-meigetsu* (literally, "potato harvest moon") indicates that people had celebrated the harvest of taro, which was imported from southeast Asia, before the arrival of rice farming. Over time this festival came to celebrate the rice harvest. Moon viewing events in the Imperial court were associated with harvest festivals in farming villages, eventually becoming the *Jugoya* festival. Offerings for the moon include Japanese pampas grass, taros, rice dumplings, and rice cakes. Interestingly, it was understood that children had silent approval to steal these offerings—people believed that the more such offerings were stolen, the more abundant the family's crops would be in the following year.

124

菊文様

Chrysanthemums pattern

きく

中国の黄河源流にある山奥の甘谷で、菊の群生地を流れてくる沢の水を飲めば長生きができるという。こうした伝説が我が国に伝えられて、よく知られる「菊水」の故事や能「菊慈童」の原典になっている。そんな菊が我が国に伝わったのは奈良時代で、平安時代には九月九日の重陽の節句には秋の菊花を愛でて詩を詠み、菊の花びらを浸した菊酒を飲んで長寿と健康を祈った。南北朝時代には菊紋が皇室の御紋とされ、秋ばかりでなく日本を代表する花となる。

In Gangu prefecture, located at the head of the Yellow River in China, a legend recounts how mountain water that flows through a clump of chrysanthemums will bestow long life. This famous legend, known as *Kiku-sui*, was introduced to Japan and became a source for the traditional Noh drama *Kiku-jido*. The chrysanthemum plant was first imported to Japan in the Nara period. In the Heian period, people enjoyed the chrysanthemum flowers immensely, writing poems about them and drinking herbal *sake* flavored with the flower's petals, hoping for long life and good health during the chrysanthemum festival. In the period of the northern and southern dynasties, the chrysanthemum design became the family crest of the Imperial court; as a result, the chrysanthemum came to be viewed as the symbolic flower of Japan.

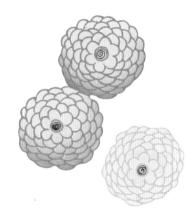

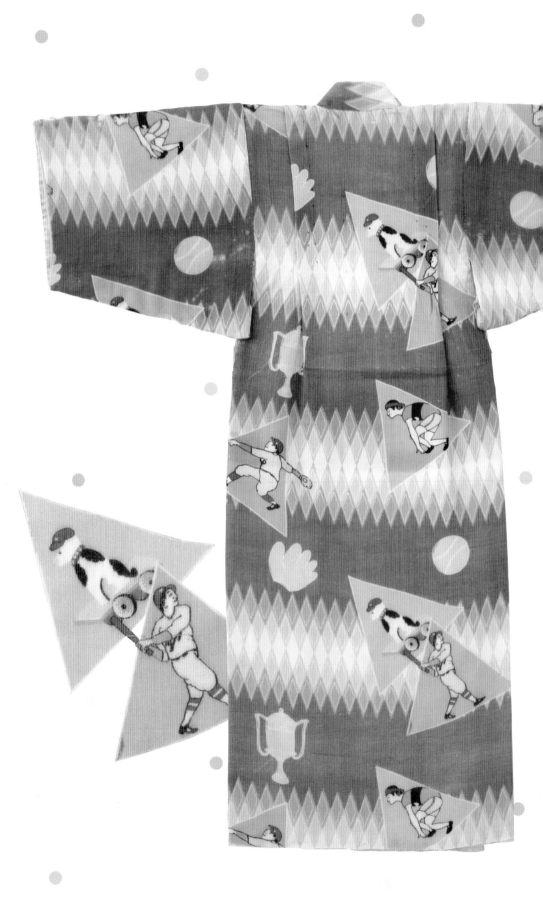

日本の小学校で運動会が始まったのは明治時代の中頃である。現在も子供たちの一年のうちの最大の学校行事として続いてきている。運動会はまた児童のみならず、父兄をも含めた地域の力を結集する成果を上げ、日本が近代国家として形成するのにも大きく役立った。野球は明治初年に伝わり、学生野球から始まって人気のスポーツとなった。

Japanese elementary schools began having "field days" in the mid-Meiji period and this is still the biggest event of the school year. Field day events helped increase a sense of unity, not only among children but also among parents and the local community. These events also played a significant role in making the Japanese nation into a modern state. Baseball was imported in the first year of the Meiji period, beginning as a school sport before taking off nationwide.

運動会文様

Field day pattern

うんどうかい

葉を落とし枯れ萎れ、多くの植物が眠りにつく冬。寒さのなか彩りを見せてくれるのは常緑の樹々草々の深い緑だろう。また、雪の白にあざやかに点じられた名残の実にはっとさせられることもある。この寒中をつき、ためらいがちに開く花々の薄みの色は、まもない冬の終わりを告げ、やがて訪れる春の到来を予祝する。

Leaves fall and plants die in winter, the sleeping season. Only the deep green of the evergreen trees adds a touch of color to the desolate winter scene. Still, bright fruits remaining on boughs can surprise us, in a sudden beautiful contrast against the snow. The light colors of flowers that bloom in winter remind us of the hope of the coming spring.

山茶花色

Sazanka iro

さざんか

やや紫みの薄い紅色。桜色よりいくぶ
ん濃いめ。山茶花はもともと四国・九州
以南の暖地の山野に自生したツバキ科
の常緑小高木で、秋から冬にかけて一
重、八重の白・ピンク・紅色の美しい花
を咲かせる。椿にくらべて花が小さく、
はらはらと花を散らし、冬の貴重な花
木として愛される。庭園や特に生け垣
として広く植えられ、童謡「たきび」の
歌詞でも馴染みである。

This is a light pink tinted with purple,
darker than *sakura iro* (the color of
cherry flowers). *Sazanka* is an
evergreen plant in the theaceous
family, and grows naturally in warm
regions such as the Shikoku and
Kyushu districts. This plant bears
single- or double-petaled flowers in
white, pink, and red. The flower is
smaller than the camellia, and scatters
its petals gracefully; this tree is very
popular as one of few that flower in
winter. This plant is very common in
home gardens, especially in hedges, as
recounted in the children's winter-
themed song "*Takibi*" (bonfire).

やや暗い濃い紅色。深紅（しんく）。南天は中国大陸原産のメギ科の常緑低木で、南天竺（なんてんじく）から渡来したとの説からこの名前がある。初夏、茎先に総状の花を咲かせ、晩秋から冬にかけて7mmほどの丸く赤い実をたくさんつける。色名はこの実の色。「難を転ずる」に通じ縁起のよい木とされ、玄関先や家の東北に鬼門封じに植えられるほか、葉は赤飯の腐敗を知らせるための飾りとして使われる。濃い緑の葉に赤い実がよく映え、雪を被った姿も美しい。

A darkish or deep red. *Nanten* is an evergreen berberidaceous shrub, native to China. The name comes from *Nantenjiku*, the region from which this plant is believed to have been imported. In early summer, this plant bears raceme flowers at the top of its stems, producing clusters of 7-mm nuts from late autumn to winter. *Nanten iro* is the color of these nuts. Considered to be a good luck symbol based on wordplay linking 'nanten' with 'a change in adverse conditions' (*nan* means 'difficulty' and *ten* means 'convert'), *nanten* is planted as a lucky charm at the entrance or northeast corner (known as the "devil's gate") of a house to ward off evil. Its leaves are also used as decoration for red rice. The red nuts contrast beautifully against dark green leaves and are also particularly lovely when covered with snow.

南天色

Nanten iro

なんてん

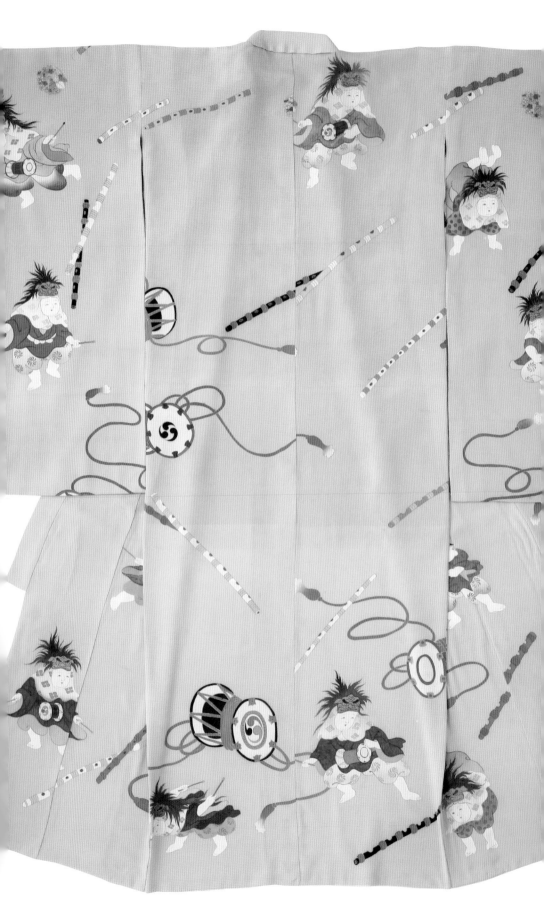

臘梅色

Roubai iro

ろうばい

黄みの濃い薄茶色。黄朽葉（きくちば）色に近い。臘月（12月）に花を咲かせるから臘梅とも呼び、花に蝋細工のような光沢があることから蝋梅ともいわれる。中国原産のロウバイ科の落葉低木で梅とは別種。冬、葉に先立って芳香のある黄色い花を咲かせる。中国ではその香りが愛されるが、日本では、花の少ない、冬季に咲く黄の花色を愛でて、庭園などに植えられる。別名、唐梅、南京梅。

Yellowish light-brown, close to *Kichikuba iro. Roubai* is a deciduous calycanthaceae shrub and is native to China. The Japanese *kanji* character for a plum appears in this name, but this plant is different from a plum tree. The name "*roubai*" is said to derive from the season in which this plant blooms, *rougetsu* (the last month of the Chinese lunar calendar), although some say it comes from its shiny, wax-like surface (*rou* means "wax" in Japanese). Fragrant yellow flowers bloom before its leaves bud. Chinese people love this plant for its aroma, while the Japanese are fond of its yellow color, a beautiful addition to an otherwise monotonous winter landscape. This shrub is also called *kara-ume* or *Nanking-ume.*

寒木瓜色

Kanboke iro

かんぼけ

あざやかな黄みの赤。茜と灰汁で染めた赤、緋（ひ）とほぼ同色。木瓜はバラ科の落葉低木で、普通は春、梅の後に白・緋・紅色の五弁の花を咲かせるが、特に冬から初春に花をつける早咲種を寒木瓜と称している。一株の色の咲き分けやぼかしなど品種も多い。直線を組み合わせたような枝振りに、葉に先立って花を咲かせる姿が面白く、夏目漱石など文人にも愛された花木である。

A bright yellowish-red, almost the same as scarlet dye made with madder and lye. *Boke*, or flowering quince, is a deciduous rosaceous shrub, generally bearing five-petaled flowers in white, scarlet, and ruby red in spring, following the plum blossom. An early flowering variety is called *kanboke* (winter quince). This plant has many varieties, some bearing multi-colored flowers on a single tree and others yielding flowers in gradations of color. The unique appearance of this plant, with flowers blooming on its rectilinear branches before the leaves bud, appealed in particular to writers such as Soseki Natsume.

橘色

Tachibana iro

たちばな

緑みの黄色。橘は日本原産の柑橘類の一種で、初夏に白い花を咲かせ、冬、黄色い果実を熟させる。実は酸味が強く種が多いので食用にしない。その芳香から魔を祓う霊果とされ、『古事記』には常世の国に生える不死を得る実の非時香菓（ときじくのかくのこのみ）として登場するほか、宮中紫宸殿の南庭に右近の橘として植えられた。また、吉祥木として賜姓の橘姓、家紋にも使われてきた。

Greenish yellow. *Tachibana* is a native citrus of Japan. Its white flowers bloom in early summer and its yellow fruit ripens in winter. As these citrus fruits are very sour and full of seeds, they are not suitable for eating. The fruit was nevertheless considered to be sacred and its fragrance was believed to ward off evil; it was even described as a heavenly fruit of immortality in the Record of Ancient Matters. *Tachibana* was also ceremonially planted in the southern garden of the *Shishinden* palace. This auspicious plant shares its name with the aristocratic Tachibana family, whose crest features an image of this flower and its leaves.

北山杉色

Kitayama-sugi iro

きたやますぎ

やや黄みを帯びた深い緑。常緑樹の葉
色で、常磐（ときわ）色より暗い。杉は日
本特産のスギ科の常緑針葉樹。重要な
林業樹種として多く植栽され、日本海
側の多雪地帯に広く分布している。京
都北山、清滝川沿いに植林された杉は
北山杉と呼ばれ、木曾檜などと並んで
日本有数の美林を形づくる。真っ直ぐ
で白い肌目をもつ北山杉は磨き丸太に
され、床柱や茶室建築に尊ばれる。

Dark green with a hint of yellow,
darker than *tokiwa-iro* (the color of
evergreen leaves). *Sugi*, or Japanese
cedar, is an evergreen tree with needle
leaves that is native to Japan. *Sugi* is
actively planted by the forestry service
as one of the most important varieties
of evergreens, and is widely
distributed in the snowy regions along
the Sea of Japan. *Sugi* planted along
the Kiyotaki River in Kitayama,
Kyoto, is specifically called *Kitayama-
sugi*, forming one of the most beautiful
forests in the country, along with the
Kiso-hinoki (forest of *hinoki* cypress in
the Kiso area). The wood of
Kitayama-sugi has a pure-white
surface and is polished into beautiful
round logs for ornamental columns
and other architectural elements of
tea-ceremony houses.

やや青みを帯びた深い緑。石蕗はキク
科の常緑の多年草で、名前の由来は艶
(つや)のある蕗という意味。葉の形は
蕗に似るが、厚みがあり、冬に枯れる
いわゆる蕗と違い通年青々とした葉を
茂らせている。別名、橐吾(つわ)。野
生のものを庭に移してもよく育ち、茶庭
によく植えられている。初冬に花茎を
伸ばし菊に似た黄色い花を咲かせ、昔
から俳人に「つわの花」として好まれ、
句にもよく詠まれてきた。

Dark green tinted with blue.
Tsuwabuki, or crested leopard, is a
perennial evergreen herb in the
asteraceous family. *Tsuwa* is derived
from *tsuya* (gloss) and *buki* is from *fuki*
(butterbur). The plant resembles the
butterbur in the shape of its leaves, but
the *tsuwabuki* leaves are thicker and
lush year-round. The plant is also
called *tsuwa*. The wild variety can be
adapted to home gardens, and is
common in gardens attached to tea-
ceremony houses. Flowering stalks
grow in early winter and bear yellow
daisy-like flowers called "*tsuwa-no-
hana*" (flowers of *tsuwa*). These
flowers, noted for their beauty, appear
frequently in poems.

石蕗色

Tsuwabuki iro

つわぶき

弾み玉色

Hazumi-dama iro

はずみだま

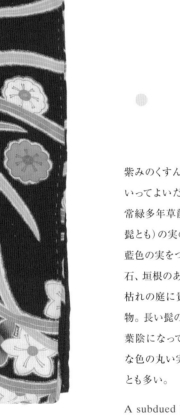

紫みのくすんだ青。ほぼ藍（あい）色といってよいだろう。弾み玉はユリ科の常緑多年草龍の髭（リュウノヒゲ、蛇の髭とも）の実のことで、冬に瑠璃色から藍色の実をつける。龍の髭は庭木や庭石、垣根のあしらいに広く用いられ、冬枯れの庭に貴重な緑を添えてくれる植物。長い髭のような葉を垂らして、その葉陰になって見えにくいが、あざやかな色の丸い実を発見して驚かされることも多い。

A subdued blue tinted with purple, almost the same color as *ai* (indigo blue). *Hazumi–dama* is the nuts of a dwarf lilyturf (*ryu-no-hige* or *hebi-no-hige* in Japanese), a perennial liliaceae plant. The winter fruit varies in color from lazuline to indigo blue. This plant is used as decoration beside garden trees and stones or around hedges, adding fresh green color to desolate winter scenes. Its round berries are startlingly bright and pretty behind the long, thin leaves.

145

黄みの白。生絹を練ってしなやかにした糸や織物の色合、練（ねり）色とほぼ同じ。梅は中国原産のバラ科の落葉高木で、日本には奈良時代以前に渡来。梅の名は中国音「（ン）メイ」をそのまま使用した音読みである。姿と香りが愛され、また実を食用にしたために広く普及し、中世までは「花」が桜ではなく梅を指す時代もあった。白梅は冬から初春、紅梅に先立って咲き、『万葉集』では雪に譬えられて多く歌われている。

白梅色

Hakubai iro

はくばい

This white has a hint of yellow, almost the same as *neri iro*, the color of softened wild silk. *Hakubai* are "white plums." The plum is a deciduous rosaceous tree, brought from China before the Nara period. Plums are called *ume* in Japanese, phonetically based on the Chinese word for this fruit, *mei*. People have long appreciated its beauty, aroma, and taste, rendering this plant even more popular and widespread. The word *hana* (flower) used to connote plums before the Middle Ages, while today the word generally suggests cherry blossoms. *Hakubai*, used as a metaphor for snow in the Anthology of Ten Thousand Leaves, blooms from winter to early spring, followed by *kobai* (red plums).

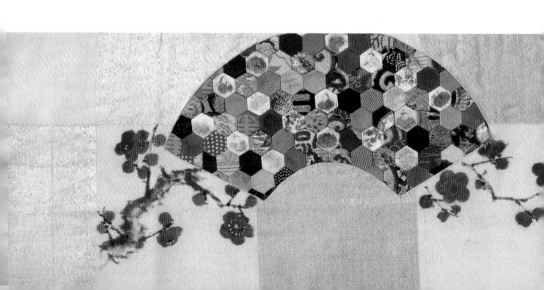

猫柳色

Nekoyanagi iro

ねこやなぎ

紫みを帯びた銀色。猫柳はヤナギ科の落葉低木カワヤナギの別名で、日本各地の水辺に自生している。2月、柳の仲間のうちで最も早く、葉に先立って白い毛に覆われた銀色の花穂をつける。その柔らかい花穂の毛が猫の毛に譬えられた。早春、陽光と水面の光とあいまって銀色に輝く姿は日本人に古くから愛されてきた。

Silver with a hint of purple. *Nekoyanagi* is a nickname for *kawayanagi*, a deciduous salicaceous tree that grows naturally on waterfronts throughout Japan. This plant bears fluffy silver buds before its leaves emerge in February, the earliest among the salicaceous family. Named for its soft fluffy buds, which resemble cat fur, *Nekoyanagi* (literally, "pussy willow") has long been appreciated by the Japanese for its shiny appearance, glimmering with reflected sunshine by the water's edge.

正月

正月はその年の豊作や、家族の健康を約束してくれる歳神をお迎えして祝う行事である。正月に飾る門松やしめ飾り、鏡餅などもすべて歳神への歓迎の意味から生じた。また正月に行われる子どもの遊びにも、子どもの健やかな成長を願いが込められているものが多い。たとえば正月の遊びとして代表的な羽根つきの羽根に使われるムクロジの実は「無患子」と書き、子どもが患わないという魔除けに通じるものとして、遊び自体に厄払いの意味が込められている。そのため、女の子の初正月に羽子板を贈る風習が生まれた。打ち損じると顔に墨を塗るのも魔除けのおまじないから転じている。

また凧あげも昔から「立春の季に空に向くは養生のひとつ」との謂れから、正月の遊びとして定着した。

The New Year's ceremony is an event to welcome the gods who bestow the annual abundant harvest and who look after the family's health throughout the year. New Year's decorations such as *shime-kazari* (straw rope), *kado-matsu* (pine branches), and *kagami-mochi* (rice cakes) originate from the ornaments originally designed to welcome these gods. Most New Year's practices symbolize hope for the well-being of children. *Hanetsuki* (Japanese badminton), for example, was associated with warding off evil, as its shuttlecock is made out of a soapberry nut, or *mukuroji* and the kanji character for this plant literally means "no child gets sick." This is how the custom began of giving *hanetsuki* racquets (*hagoita*) to girls on their first New Year's Day. It's interesting to note that when playing *hanetsuki*, anyone who misses the shuttlecock has his or her face smeared with ink. This is also derived from a ritual to ward off evil. Flying kites also became popular as a New Year's pastime, as it was said that looking up to the sky on the first day of the year, which marks the beginning of spring in the lunar calendar, promotes good health.

孟宗の筍文様

Moso's bamboo shoots pattern

もうそうのたけのこ

古今の孝行談を集めた『二十四孝』の伝記が中国にある。その一つに、3世紀の呉の人・孟宗は、病気の母親が冬の最中に筍を望み、雪降る中を出かけて探すが見つからず。天に願って涙すると、雪が解けて筍が生えてきたという、老父に酒を飲ませたい一念で、滝の水を酒に変えたという日本の養老伝説と対照される孝行談の故事がある。雪中に筍を堀る孟宗や、雪が積もる竹藪に笠と鍬を添えて描かれる文様は孝行に育つ子を願う親の欲目か、子供の衣装によく見られる。良質の筍が採れる「孟宗竹」の謂れでもある。

The Chinese biographical collection entitled *Nijushikou* (or "24 Filial Pieties") is a series of stories of remarkable sons. One such story tells of a man named *Moso* from the Wu kingdom, searching for a bamboo shoot in a snowstorm for his sick mother. Despairing of his search, he cries out; the snow melts away, suddenly revealing a bamboo shoot. This story is often compared to the Japanese legend of *Yoro,* in which a man changes a waterfall into *sake* for his aging father. A pattern depicting *Moso* digging for bamboo shoots in the snow, or a pattern of a snowy bamboo grove along with a braided hat and a grub hoe, was drawn on children's kimono, in the hopes that these images would cause the children to be properly filial and respectful.

春の七草文様

Seven herbs of
spring pattern

はるのななくさ

正月七日の人日（じんじつ）は、五節句の一つ。この日は春の野に出て若菜を摘み、それを食して邪気を祓い、一年の健康を願った。古くは宮中行事だったこの節句行事も次第に民間へ広まり、七種（七草）粥の習慣となった。粥に入れる若菜を「春の七草」と呼び、芹、薺（なずな）、御行、はこべら、仏の座、すずな（蕪）、すずしろ（大根）で、これらの菜を細かく叩いて粥に入れる。そのことの「薺打つ」が新年の季語になっている。七草を叩く包丁と俎、擂木を添えて、「ままごと」遊びを思わせる子供服らしい図柄である。

The Feast of the Seven Herbs of Health is one of five traditional seasonal events. On this day, people picked spring herbs from the fields and cooked rice porridge with these herbs to ward off evil. This custom began in the Imperial court and later spread to the public as the Feast of the Seven Herbs of Health. The seven herbs include *seri, nazuna, gogyo, hakobera, hotokenoza, suzuna,* and *suzushiro*. These herbs are chopped and put in rice porridge. The saying *nazuna-utsu* (or "chopping herbs"), thus became a poetic seasonal phrase reflecting the New Year. A knife, a cutting board, and a pestle remind us of children playing house, pretending to prepare this Feast, and is a cherished motif for children's kimonos.

儀式と着物の様式

Kimono and Ceremonies

宮参り

Miya-mairi (Visiting a Shinto shrine)

生後初めて産土（うぶすな）神の氏神
に参拝させる行事。男児なら生後三十
一日目、女児なら三十三日目に宮参り
させるのが一般的だが、七十五日目、
百日目という地方もある。三十日前後
というのは母子ともに健康となり、外出
も無理のない頃である。父方の祖母や
産婆が赤ん坊を神社に連れていった
が、現在では両親とともに参るほうが
普通だろう。宮参りの祝い着は母方の
里から贈られるのが習わしで、男児に
は熨斗目模様に兜や鷹、女児なら華や
かな模様友禅というあたりが伝統的。
背縫いのない「一つ身」の着物で、祝
い着の紐には犬張子、でんでん太鼓な
どの縁起物をゆわえつけることもある。
神社に行く前に男児なら鍋墨、女児な
ら紅で額に犬の字や×を書いたり、神
前で子どもをわざと泣かせるという習
慣も残る。

Miya-mairi is a child's first visit to a local Shinto shrine at which an *ubusuna* god is worshipped. Parents generally take a baby boy to the shrine on the thirty-first day after birth and a girl on the thirty-third day, but in some regions the tradition takes place on the seventy-fifth or hundredth day after birth. The date was reportedly set around the thirtieth day following childbirth, as by approximately this time the mother and baby are physically stable enough to go out. In the olden times, the grandmother on the paternal side or a midwife used to take the child to the shrine, but today the parents commonly take their babies. The ceremonial kimono for *miya-mairi* is customarily sent by the family on the maternal side. Traditionally, a kimono with a *samurai* warrior helmet or hawk patterns in combination with a *noshime* design is sent to a baby boy and a bright-patterned *yuzen* kimono is sent to a baby girl. The kimono is called a hitotsu-mi (referring to a type of tailoring for babies). Lucky charms such as dog-shaped dolls or toy-drum-shaped accessories are sometimes tied to the strings of the ceremonial kimono. Before going to the shrine, some people customarily depict a *kanji* character of "dog" or a cross mark on the child's forehead–using ash from a cooking pan for boys, or in rouge for girls. The custom of making babies cry in front of the altar also still remains in some areas.

宮参りの着物
女児

The Kimono of Miya-mairi
Girl

宮参りの着物

男児

The Kimono of Miya-mairi
Boy

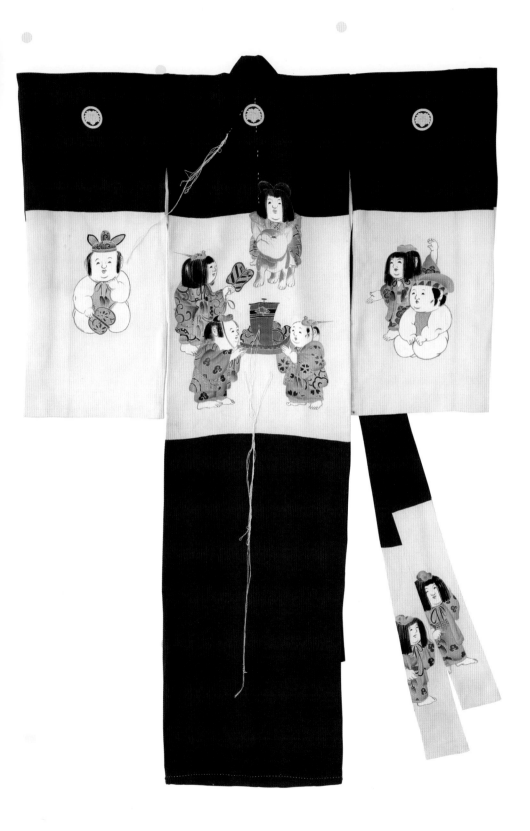

あぶちゃんと宮参り帽

Abu-chan and miyamairi cap

あぶちゃんとは涎掛けのことで、お宮参りや、お食い初め（※注）などの通過儀礼の際に、晴れ着とともに用いたものである。また宮参りの際に使用する宮参り帽と対にして作られたものもある。それぞれ、乳児の健康や魔除け、将来を祝福するため、赤色や吉祥紋様を尽くして可愛らしく仕立てられた。中でも鯛を象ったものは、お食い初めの儀式に使用された物だと思われる。また頭巾の後方に兜の吹替えしのように二枚のしころ布を垂らした帽子は、男児の宮参り帽として、江戸から明治期にかけてしころ頭巾を参考に作られたものではないだろうか。

※注　お食い初め
一生食べ物に困らないことを願い、生後100日目頃の歯が生えはじめた時期に行われる祝いの行事。新しい茶碗や汁椀を用いて赤飯や尾頭付きの魚などの馳走を用意し、食べる真似をさせる。また歯が石のように固く丈夫になることを願い小石をそなえることもある。

A *miyamairi* cap and an *abu-chan* (baby's bib) are used in rites such as the miyamairi shrine visit or the ceremony known as *okuizome**. The color red and auspicious patterns are used abundantly to adorn these items, warding off evil and—hopefully—ensuring the baby's good health and future success. An *abu-chan* with a red sea bream pattern generally seems to have been used in the *okuizome* ceremony. The boy's cap has two pieces of cloth that attach to and hang from the edge of the cap, covering the nape of the neck. It would appear that this type of cap was created in the Edo or Meiji period, given the resemblance of the design to a hood worn in those days.

Note * Okuizome
This is a ceremony celebrated around the hundredth day after birth, when a baby's teeth are coming in, in the hopes of ensuring that the baby will always have enough to eat, throughout his or her life. In this event, festive red rice and grilled whole fish are prepared using brand-new bowls and plates, and people pretend to feed the babies. In some cases, little stones are displayed along with the dishes to symbolize hopes for sound and healthy teeth.

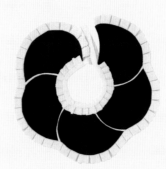

あぶちゃんと宮参り帽

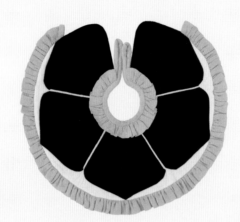

背守りと迷子札

幼児の一つ身の着物の背にお守りとして縫い付けた飾り縫い、または飾り紋のこと。桃山時代ころから行われ、「背の縫い目のない着物を着ると魔がさす」といい、そのためにお守りとしてつけたといわれる。宮参りの祝着には正式とされる「守り縫い」を、通常の着物には四菱紋や折鶴を糸で縫ったり、縮緬細工の押し絵風の切付繍の飾りをつけたりした。また裏に名前と住所を記してある押絵細工を振り下げて迷子札を兼ねた例もある。

「守り縫い」の縫い端を長く垂らして縫い放しにするのは、子どもが長寿であることの願いと、魔物に教われても魔物がこの糸を引き抜いて子どもが無事だという謂れから。一説に、子どもが火や水に落ちたとき、産神がこれを引っ張って助ける紐だともいわれる(※「守り縫い」についてはP164~167のお宮参りの着物参照)。

Semamori (literally, "back protection") is a decorative embroidery or appliqué applied to the back of an infant's kimono for luck. *Semamori* began to appear in the Momoyama period based on the belief that evil spirits can enter a body from the back if the kimono has no stitches on this surface (baby kimono are so small that fabric swatches don't need to be sewn together). Formal *mamori-nui* stitches were sewn into the ceremonial kimono worn on the shrine visit. For daily kimono, the *yotsubishi* symbol or an origami crane would be sewn on the back. Some people would stitch on a padded appliqué resembling a work of the *chirimen* craft, while others would attach *oshie*, or raised designs with a child's name and address written on the back for identification.

For the formal *mamori-nui*'s the long ends of the threads are left uncut and hang loose, for long life-based on the belief that if devils were to attack and try to kidnap a child, they would grab these threads and the child would escape. Some say that *Ubugami* (the god of birth) will save a child from drowning or from burns in a fire by pulling the child free using these threads. (See the kimono on p.164~ 167 for *mamori-nui*.)

七五三

Shichi-Go-San

現在、七五三と呼び習わす宮参りの行事は、もともと吉日に行うという以外は日が定まっておらず、それぞれの子どもの成長に合わせた別の行事だった。三歳は髪置きの祝いで、切ったり剃ったりしていた髪を伸ばしはじめる儀式、五歳は男女とも着物の付け紐を外し、帯を初めて結ぶ帯解きの祝いだったが、後に五歳男児は袴着の祝いとなり、帯解きは七歳女児の祝いとなった。十一月十五日という日が決められたのは、江戸時代、五代将軍徳川綱吉の子徳松の袴着の祝い日に由来するとも、また秋の氏神の収穫祭の日に合わせたともいわれる。それが三歳五歳七歳を一緒に祝うようになるのは江戸時代も後半のことであり、七五三の名称も明治になって東京で言われはじめたものらしい。現在、伝統的といわれる七五三の宮参りの晴れ着は、三歳女児は初宮参りの祝い着に被布、五歳男児は熨斗目模様の紋付に羽織袴、七歳女児が本裁ち友禅の振袖に帯を締め扱（しごき）を着け、懐に筥迫（はこせこ）を入れたものである。

Shichi-Go-San (literally "seven-five-three") is a rite to celebrate the passage of children into middle childhood. People used to visit Shinto shrines on any auspicious day, and this rite was not attached to a fixed date in ancient times. For three-year-olds, people held a ceremony known as *kamioki*. Beginning on this day, children would begin to grow their hair; prior to this ceremony, their heads would be shaven or their hair would be very short. For five-year-olds, people celebrated the *obi-toki* ceremony, in which children would stop wearing the traditional children's sash and begin to use an obi for the first time with a kimono. Later, the *obi-toki* ceremony became an event for seven-year-old girls, while five-year-old boys participated in a ceremony in which they were allowed to wear a ceremonial skirt for the first time. In the Edo period, the date of these ceremonies was fixed on the fifteenth day of the eleventh month in the lunar calendar. This date is believed to commemorate the day on which the son of the fifth Shogun *Tsunayoshi Tokugawa* wore a ceremonial skirt for the first time. The date was also said to have been established to fall near the time of a number of autumn harvest festivals. It was in the late Edo period that people started to combine the ceremonies for three-, five-, and seven-year-olds. It is believed that the festival came to be called *Shichi Go San* in Tokyo beginning in the Meiji period.

七五三の着物

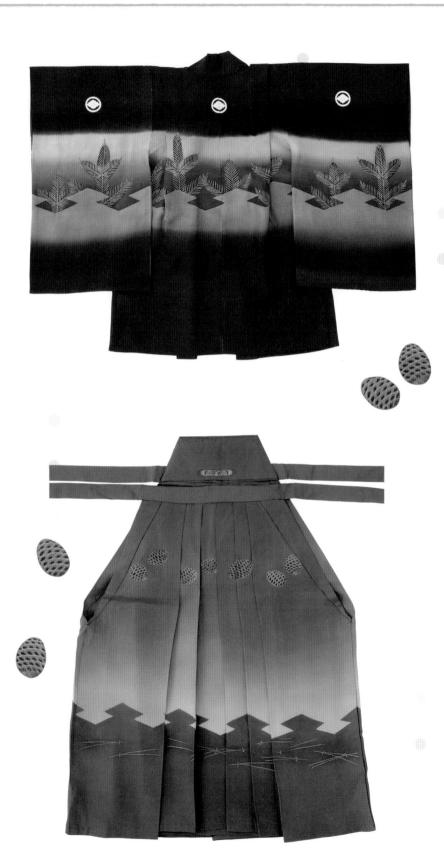

飾り縫い

Kazari-nui (ornamental embroidery)

子どもの長着を着やすくするためと、着物の着崩れを防ぐための付け紐の縫合部に施す装飾をかねた刺繍。輪鼓（りゅうご）文や折鶴などの吉祥文が施された。一つ身の付け紐は半幅または三つ割にして袋に縫い、躾をかけた。また付け紐のとじ糸は古くは黄、または赤色を用いて縫い、紐と異色の糸を使用した。

Ornamental embroidery of auspicious patterns–such as the ryugo-mon symbol and the origami crane pattern–were applied at the joint of sashes. A strip of cloth was folded in two or three and sewn to make a simple sash to attach to a hitotsu-mi baby kimono. In the olden days, the sash would be sewn using red or yellow thread, to contrast with the sash cloth.

被布と道行

十歳以下の少女が着る被布は「袖無し被布（ひふ）」と呼ばれ、大人用の被布と違って袖がなく、菊結びの絹紐飾りが打ち合わせ部の両肩に縫い付けられている。また衿は被布衿と呼ばれる衿肩を丸く仕立てた小衿がつく。室内着なので縮緬（ちりめん）、綸子（りんず）、繻子（しゅす）など高級絹織物で仕立てることが多い。江戸中期に公家の童女の間で外衣として着られたが、やがて屋内防寒用となり、一般にも広まった。もともとは男子用だったが、江戸後期には女性に、また明治には子どもにも普及した。道行（みちゆき）は被布に似ていて袖があるものをさし、衿は細身かつ角形の「道行き衿」に作られている。

Hifu worn by girls under ten years old are called "sleeveless *hifu*." Silk braids adorn the chest. The hifu has a small round collar called a *hifu-eri*. This garment is for indoor use, and so is made from luxurious silks: *chirimen* (a silk fabric with fine wrinkles), or *linzu* or *shusu* (silks featuring fine woven patterns), for example. *Hifu* were worn by girls of noble court families as outer coats in the mid-Edo period. Eventually, use as indoor winter clothing spread among the common people. Originally the garment was for boys, but in the late Edo period, it came to be worn by women, subsequently becoming popular as children's clothes in the Meiji period. *Michiyuki*, on the other hand, is similar to the *hifu*, but with sleeves and a thin, square collar.

十三参り

Jusan mairi (temple visit for thirteen-year-olds)

旧暦三月十三日（現在は四月十三日）、その年に数えで十三歳になった子どもが虚空蔵菩薩（こくうぞうぼさつ）に参詣して、知恵と福を授けてもらう行事。「知恵もらい」ともいわれる関西中心の行事である。虚空蔵菩薩はいわゆる十三仏の十三番目の仏で縁日も十三日、これに十三歳をちなませたもので、安永二年（1773）に始まったとされて起源は新しい。古来、十三歳は成年式の行われる年齢で、これに虚空蔵の縁日を結びつけたものらしい。最も有名なのが「嵯峨の虚空蔵さん」と呼ばれる京都嵐山の法輪寺の十三参り。帰途、渡月橋を渡り終える前に振り返ると授った知恵が返ってしまうと言い伝えられている。女児はこの参詣に初めて大人用の地一反の着物を拵えて身に着けるので、折から花の盛り、両親に連れられた子どもの衣裳くらべのような華やかな行事となる。

On the thirteenth day of the third month of the lunar calendar (now April 13), children in their 13th year (with this age counted using the old Japanese method) go to a temple to pray before *Kokuzo-bosatsu (Akasa-garbha)* in order to be bestowed with wisdom and happiness. This event, also called *chie-morai* (literally, "bestowed with wisdom") is common around the Kansai district. This ceremony is associated with *Kokuzo-bosatsu*, the thirteenth of a particular series of thirteen Buddhas, and a street fair dedicated to this Buddha, held on the thirteenth day of the month. *Jusan mairi* is said to have started in 1773. Additionally, the age of 13 was a traditional age for initiation ceremonies. The *Jusan mairi* visit to the *Horinji* temple in Saga, Kyoto (known as *Saga no Kokuzo-san*), is the most famous. Legend has it that if you turn around and look back before you cross the *Togetsukyo* Bridge on the way home from the temple, you will lose the wisdom you gained inside. On the visit to temple, girls are on display in new ceremonial kimono (using the same amount of fabric as an adult kimono, for the first time), such that this flamboyant event–in the middle of the blossoming season–often seems like a children's kimono contest.

十三参りの着物

普段着

Everyday kimono

上流階級の子どもの普段着は、絹素材を使用した絣や銘仙など華やかで可愛らしいものが多い。また庶民の子も、よそ行きのモスリン友禅のポンチ柄から、綿縞、綿絣の普段着を着て精一杯に遊んでいた。第二次大戦後は暮らしの変化から、ウールの着物が銘仙や木綿にとって代わられた。

Children of the upper classes used to wear luxurious and beautiful *kasuri* or *meisen* kimono made from silk. On the other hand, children from ordinary families would wear cotton striped kimono and cotton *kasuri*-patterned kimono as everyday wear. Ordinary children would sometimes wear muslin *yuzen* kimono as holiday attire. After WW II, *meisen* and cotton kimonos were replaced by wool kimono, corresponding with changing lifestyles.

着物の文様
Child Kimonos Pattern

鳩文様
Dove pattern

はと

古来、鳥は天と地を行き交う生き物としてよく表されたが、鳩が鳥文様に描かれるのは少なく、多くは近代になってからである。しかし、我が国では古くから「鳩に三枝の礼あり」と、子鳩が親鳩の三枝下に止まることの礼節が説かれ、また八幡大将軍神社の神使として、鳩が戦いの守りとされていた。また近代でも、軍国の思いを秘めながらも平和の鳩をかざして、多くの子供の衣装に描かれたのが実情であった。そんな鳩が、戦況の難を転じて勝利に導く意で南天と共に表されている。

Long ago, birds were seen as creatures capable of coming and going between heaven and earth, but doves were rarely depicted in bird patterns, and began to appear only in modern times. Nonetheless, doves are not unknown to history–there is an old Japanese saying that doves are polite, in that young doves typically roost below the elder doves. These birds were originally considered to be the embodiment of the guardian god of battles, enshrined in the Yawata Taishogun shrine. In modern days, doves, though a symbol of peace, were often drawn on children's kimono to convey a sense of patriotism, even a hint of militarism. Doves were drawn on kimono along with the nanten plant, the symbol of a change in adverse conditions and the hope for an upset victory.

薬玉文様

Kusudama pattern

くすだま

五月五日の端午の節句に、夏に流行る疫病を封じるために菖蒲と艾を吊して邪気を祓う風習が、古代中国から伝わってあった。やがてそれは麝香（じゃこう）や沈香（じんこう）などの香料を袋に入れて、造花と共に飾って御簾や柱に掛ける「薬玉」となった。さらに、五色の紐で装飾して華麗な後世の薬玉の形が出来上がり、優美に憧れる女性心から、美しい飾り物を着物の文様として取り入れた。とくに、女児の七五三の祝い着に薬玉や茱萸袋が近代以降に文様としてよく見られる。

There is a custom, imported from China, of hanging sachets containing *shobu* and *moxa* to ward off evil and to counteract summer plagues on Boys' Day. Fine fragrances such as musk and agarwood came to be placed in sachets called *kusudama*, which decorated bamboo blinds and columns along with artificial flowers. Later, *kusudama* came to be gracefully decorated with five-colored strings and employed in kimono patterns. *Kusudama* and *gumi-bukuro* (a kind of herbal sachet) have in recent times been depicted particularly on girls' ceremonial kimono for the *Shichi-Go-San* festival for children aged seven, five and three.

几帳文様

Kicho pattern

きちょう

几帳は平安貴族の邸宅の、殺風気で広
い部屋の仕切りとして用いられた調度
飾り。二本の柱に横木を渡し、そこに
帳（とばり）を垂らしたもので、この帳に
様々な文様を描いたり織り出されてい
た。後世、憧れの王朝風俗を連想させ
る吉祥文様として、また草花や物語絵
と組み合わせて優美な意匠に仕立て
上げられていった。とくに、こうした王
朝の几帳や檜扇、薬玉などのしつらえ
を優美に合わせ描いた内裏文様を「大
内文様」と呼んでいる。

Kicho is a decorative partition used in
aristocratic homes in the Heian period.
A sheet of fabric was hung from a bar
placed between two poles and various
patterns were painted on or woven into
the fabric. In later times, *kicho* was
employed in kimono designs as an
homage to the culture of nobility, often
used in combination with grasses and
flowers or with motifs from old stories.
These images are considered
auspicious. Graceful patterns
incorporating royal objects and
accessories such as *kicho*, cypress fans,
and *kusudama* sachets may all be
categorized as *ouchi monyo* (Imperial
court pattern).

唐獅子に
牡丹文様

Lions and tree peonies
pattern

からししにぼたん

能・謡曲の「石橋」では、大江定基が出家して寂照法師と名のり、各国の仏跡霊地を巡礼する。寂照法師が中国の山深い清涼山に踏み分けて石橋を渡ろうとすると、童子が現われて千丈の谷に懸るこの石橋は苔むして滑りやすく人間は渡れないと告げる。やがて、文殊菩薩が出現して法華経を詠み、眷属の獅子が現れて牡丹に戯れ、万歳の御代を寿ぐという話である。牡丹が咲き誇る深山渓谷に懸かる石橋の上で獅子が舞う文芸文様を「石橋」といい、石橋が描かれないものを「唐獅子牡丹」と呼ぶ。

In the Noh song *Shakkyo* (The Stone Bridge), a man named *Sadamoto Oe* becomes a priest and changes his name to *Jakusho Hoshi*, performing pilgrimages to Buddhist ruins and other sacred sites. As *Jakusho Hoshi* climbs the steep mountain known as *Seiryo-zan* in China, attempting to cross a stone bridge, a child appears and stops him, saying that the moss-covered bridge was too slippery for a man to cross. Suddenly Manjushri Bodhisattva appears and recites a Buddhist sutra, while his servant lion flits and dances from one tree peony to another, celebrating long-lasting time of peace. A pattern featuring a bridge over the Miyama valley, based on this story, is called *shakkyo*. A pattern of lions and tree peonies without the bridge is referred to as *karashishi-botan*.

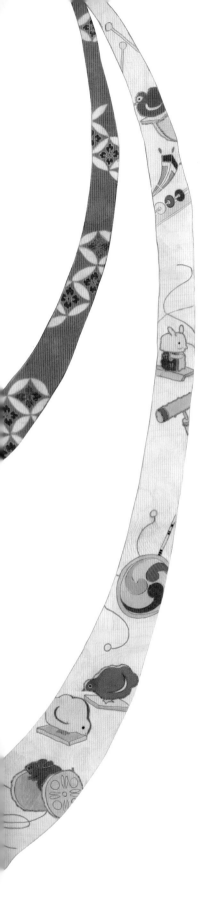

熨斗文様
Noshi pattern

のし

本来、熨斗は鮑（あわび）の肉を薄く削いで、延して乾かしたもの。儀礼用の酒肴とし、束ねて「束ね熨斗」と称した。熨すを延すの祝意で表し、進物に熨斗鮑の包形を添えるようになったのは近世のこと。それは現在でも、熨斗袋の上隅に簡略化されて跡をとどめている。この愛でたい束ね熨斗の形を華麗に装飾して意匠化したのがいわゆる熨し文様である。束ね熨斗文様ともいわれ、江戸時代の婚礼の振袖などに見られ、近代では子供の祝い着などに用いられている。男児の祝い着である熨斗目着物も、身体全体を熨斗に見立てて束ねた形を表している。

Noshi is a kind of ceremonial fold attached to gifts to express good wishes. This custom started in relatively modern times, and a simplified version of *noshi* is still attached to formal gift packages. *Noshi* originated from dried, thin-sliced abalone called *noshi-awabi*. The *noshi* pattern was inspired by the *tabane-noshi* (a bundle of ceremonial abalone snacks). This pattern is also called the *tabane-noshi* pattern and was employed in ceremonial kimono for children as well as for wedding kimono in the Edo period. *Noshime-kimono* is a type of ceremonial kimono for boys and also originated from folded *noshi*.

鶴
亀
文
様

Crane and tortoise
pattern

つ
る
か
め

松竹梅鶴亀を組み合わせて、蓬莱信仰に基づく吉祥文様とする。中国の伝説に、沙棠・琅玕・絳樹の吉祥樹が生え、神獣の龍と鳳凰が棲む神仙境の崑崙山がある。それが我が国に伝えられて何時しか松竹梅と鶴亀に置き換えられ、「蓬莱」や「松竹梅鶴亀」文様と称されるようになった。鶴と亀のみが描かれることもしばしばで、鶴は鳳凰に倣って雌雄を阿吽の形で表し、竜宮の蓑亀が描かれた。また、近世期以降は儒教精神に基づく鶴千年や亀万年の教えが説かれ、鶴の雌雄と雄の子を描いて、長子（男子）誕生を寿ぐ模様とした。

Pine, bamboo, plum, are drawn together with a crane and tortoise to form an auspicious pattern originating in a belief in *Horai* (an eternal utopia). In China, legend told of a permanent dreamland on the legendary *Kun-Lun* mountain, home to lucky plants known as *sato*, *rokan*, and *koju* and to sacred animals such as the dragon and phoenix. When this legend was introduced to Japan, the plants were replaced by pine, bamboo, and plum, and the creatures became the crane and tortoise; this pattern came to be called *Horai* or *shochikubai-tsurukame*. Some images depict a pair of cranes associated with a particular mantra, along with a tortoise covered in green algae. In recent times, a related lucky pattern featuring a crane couple with a young male crane–an image originating from Confucian writings–came to be used to celebrate the birth of a first-born son.

童話文様

Fairy tales pattern

どうわ

近代になって子供の教育用に多くの「童話」が作られだした。昔の御伽話や伝説、寓話をもとに、新しい筋書きで整えて再生され、近代的な童話が次々と生み出された。また、西洋の昔話や童話を倣って創作童話が盛んに作られた。日本の御伽話や西洋の昔話は、意外にも残酷だったり恐い話が多いのだが、それを楽しく強く、正しく優しい主人公に作り替えて近代の昔話や童話ができていった。正義感溢れる美談を尽して、国を支える子供作りに役立てようと、童話も勇壮果敢な戦争画と並べて子らの着物に描かれた。

In modern times, to educate children, new fairy tales were created based on Japanese traditional fairy stories, legends, and fables as well as on Western folk tales and fairy stories. As traditional tales were surprisingly cruel and frightening, the tales were changed to happier ones, with strong, generous heroes dispensing justice. The motifs derived from these heartwarming, highly moral stories were drawn on children's kimono, along with heroic war images in order to promote a patriotic spirit among the youth.

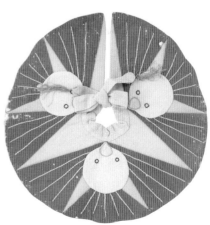

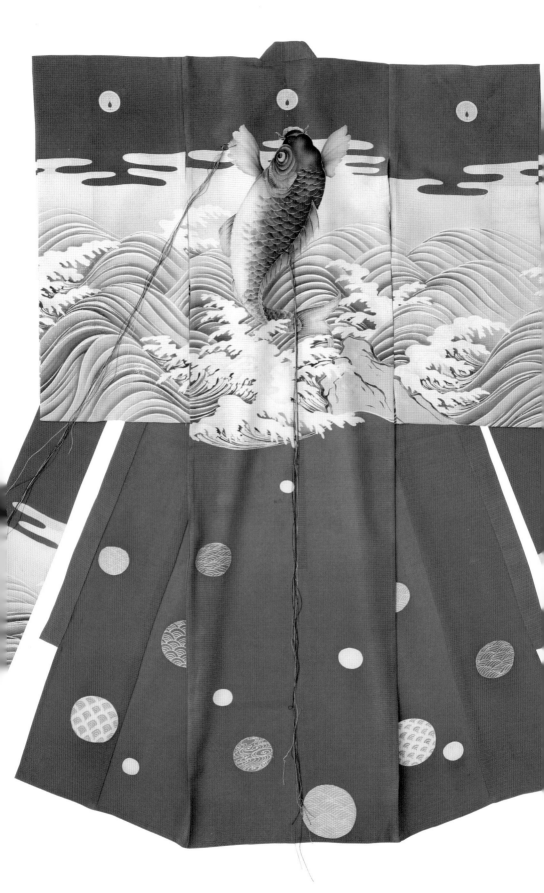

鯉文様

Carp pattern

こい

魚の中でも鯉は霊力に富む魚とされ、よく飛び跳ねることから龍に変じる出世魚とされる。中国の黄河上流にある急瀬の龍門を泳ぎ登って鯉が龍に化したといわれ、難関を極めた官吏登用の科挙試験に合格して出世する例えに用いられ、「登龍門」の言葉がある。また、鯉は魚類三百六十の最上位とされ、背に三十六枚の鱗が一列に並ぶとして「三十六鱗」や「六六魚」と称され、「六々変じて九々鱗と成る」のように八十一枚の鱗がある龍に変身するという。我が国では「鯉の滝登り」と表して、子等の健康と出世を乞い願い、端午の節句の幟や旗に、また男児誕生の祝いとして躍動感の溢れる鯉の絵が描かれる。

Carp was once believed to be a spiritual fish and even today is considered a symbol of a successful career, based on a Chinese legend in which a carp jumped over the Dragon Gate in the rapid current of the upper Yellow River, transforming into a dragon as it leapt. The legend gave rise to the phrase "toryu-mon" (gateway to success), which was used in the olden days to describe difficult employment tests for government officials. Another legend recounts how a carp is the king of 360 kinds of fish, with 36 dorsal scales; this carp then transforms into a dragon with 81 scales on its back. In Japan, a dynamic pattern of leaping carp is drawn on a boy's kimono in celebration of the birth of a baby boy, in the hopes of securing his good health and success. The patterns of carp streamers are applied on windmills and banners used in the Boy's Day ceremony.

御所人形文様
Gosho ningyo pattern

ごしょにんぎょう

古く宮中では、貴族男児の元服に際して宮中への初出参があった。その時、朝廷から人形が手土産に贈られる習慣があり、初参（ういざん）人形と呼ばれて宮中に参上する可愛い童子姿を写して作られていた。また、子供の健康と文芸の上達を願う庶民の玩具人形と合して、民間に広まっていったのが御所人形である。江戸時代に、御所人形を作っていたのが大阪の伊豆蔵屋だったことから、「伊豆蔵人形」とも呼ばれるようになる。御所人形が文様として多く描かれたのは近代で、鯉車や鳩車、鼓の玩具などと共にあどけない表情で描かれた。

Gosho ningyo used to be called *uizan ningyo*, referring to a doll representing a little boy offered as a gift on the occasion of a coming-of-age ceremony for aristocratic boys in the Imperial court. In later years, *gosho ningyo* spread among the general public as a toy offering hopes for good health and progress in learning. In the Edo period, this doll was also called *izukura ningyo*, after the name of the manufacturer in Osaka prefecture. *Gosho ningyo* came to be employed in kimono patterns in relatively recent years. These dolls were depicted to express a child's innocence, in combination with dove-shaped or carp-shaped toy cars, hand drums, and other toys.

玩具文様

Toys pattern

おもちゃ

多くは、身近にあった他愛のない物や、子の健康と成育を祈願する飾り物が子らの玩具に発展している。子供の玩具は古くから日本各地で作られ、地域の産物や生物、そして信仰に結び付いて取材されたものが多い。平安時代に中国から渡来した独楽は、喧嘩独楽やベーゴマにまで発展して、男児の人気玩具で、女児の人気はやはり手毬だった。

Children often play with small everyday items or with decorations normally used by adults to pray for children's good health and growth. Eventually these items come to be called toys. Children's toys have been manufactured all over Japan, associated with local products and creatures as well as with local religious practices. In the Heian period, spinning tops were imported from China, and play with these toys eventually developed into *kenka-goma* and *bey-goma* (a sort of "top fighting"), a popular pastime among boys. The most popular toys among girls, on the other hand, were traditional *temari* balls.

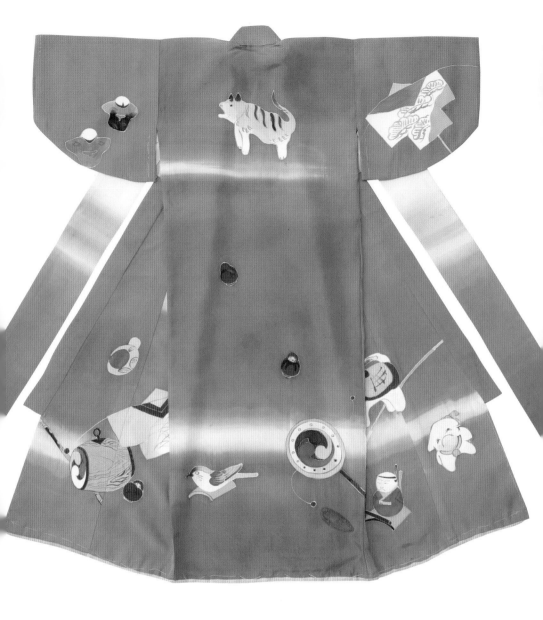

いぬ文様

Dogs pattern

いぬ

子供の誕生は嬉しいが、危険と隣り合わせだったのが昔の出産である。出産に際して母子の安全を祈り、形代として難事を移し負わせる「天児（あまがつ）」や「這子（ほうこ）」人形を、産室や乳児の枕元に置いて祓いにした。また民間では、犬が多産で御産が軽く、育て易いと安産の御守にした。そんな犬の形に子供の顔を似せて作ったのが犬筥（いぬばこ）。雌雄の犬のうずくまった形に作った蓋つきの小箱で、本来の寝所を警戒する役目と併せて魔除けや安産の祈願に用いた。犬張子も同じく、犬の立ち姿をした張子細工で宮参りの贈物とし、また三月の節句飾りに用いた。

In the old days, as giving birth was life-threatening work, *amagatsu* or *bouko* dolls were displayed by beds as a scapegoat for evil, in the hopes of ensuring the safety of the mother and child. Dogs were considered to be a symbol of fecundity, easy delivery, and easy child rearing. The dog motif was also employed in *inu-bako*, a dog-shaped box with a human face on the lid. A pair of *inu-bako*, resembling a couple of dogs, was used to guard bedrooms, to ward off evil, and as a lucky charm for easy delivery. *Inu-hariko* is also a dog-shaped doll offered as a gift on a visit to a shrine, or as a decoration for the Doll Festival.

人形文様

Dolls pattern

にんぎょう

昭和初期、米国との関係が緊張した時に、米国人の宣教師によって親善のための青い目の人形が日本の子供に贈られてきた。また、日本からも返礼の市松人形が贈られた。そんなことから、西洋人形と日本人形を並べて描かれることが多かった。また、ベッティ人形やキューピーなどのキャラクター人形が日本に運ばれてきたのも昭和初期で、モダニズムの波に乗ってはるばる海外からやってきたのを、物珍しさも手伝って子供や女性の衣服に描かれ、流行となった。

When tensions between United States and Japan heightened in the early Showa period, American missionary priests gave blue-eyed dolls to Japanese children to convey goodwill, and the Japanese returned the courtesy with traditional *ichimatsu* dolls. Based on this exchange, Western dolls and Japanese dolls were depicted side by side. Unique new dolls were also introduced to Japan in the early Showa period, along with the modernist wave. The fresh look of dolls from abroad became a popular motif on kimono for women and children.

蝶文様

Butterfly pattern

ちょう

青虫や毛虫から蛹を経て、羽化して蝶になって飛び立つ蝶。このように二度の生涯を持ち、高く飛翔することから蝶は再生や登仙を象徴する文様として表される。平安時代では貴族の車紋や織物、金具などに文様として見られ、その姿が羽を広げた形で表されて「臥蝶（ふせちょう）」と呼ばれた。また鎌倉時代では、羽を立てて止まる優美な姿の「揚羽蝶」が武家に好まれ、その勇ましさと戦場での不幸に際しても昇天を願う気持ちから武具によく用いられた。しかし、蝶は花から花へと移り気な生き物として、近代では婚礼衣装などに利用することを避けたともいわれる。藤原氏を表した藤と、貴族の好んだ蝶は平安王朝を代表的する文様である。

The butterfly is the symbol of rebirth or ascension to heaven, due to the metamorphosis this creature undergoes and its flight. Butterfly patterns were employed in aristocratic family crests applied to carriages, fabrics, and metal furniture in the Heian period. A pattern of butterflies with spread wings is called *fuse-cho*. In the Kamakura period, swallowtail butterfly patterns were used by samurai families to adorn their armor, in the hopes of rising to heaven if they were to be killed in battle. On the other hand, butterflies were also deemed a fickle creature, flitting from flower to flower. Therefore, women seem to have avoided wearing butterfly patterns at wedding ceremonies and other formal events. *Fuji* (Japanese wisteria), associated with the noble Fujiwara family, appeared as a common pattern of the Heian era, often paired with aristocracy's favorite insect, the butterfly.

貝桶文様

Kai-oke pattern

かいおけ

大きな蛤の内側に歌合わせの図柄や文様、そして歌の上と下の句を別々に記して、それをトランプの神経衰弱のように合わせて興じる「貝合せ（貝覆い）」が平安王朝の遊戯としてあり、貝を納める容器の貝桶にも贅を尽して金蒔絵や彩色がされて豪華に飾られた。また、貝が本来の一組でしか合わないことから夫婦和合の堅い契りとして表され、貝合せが大切な嫁入り道具ともなった。貝桶に睦まじく添って描かれる鴛鴦（おしどり）も夫婦円満の徴とされる文様。

Kai-oke is a container for shells used in *kai-awase*, a shell-matching game (similar to the card game "Memory") played by the nobility in the Heian period. Shells used in *kai-awase* were beautifully decorated with various matching motifs or with matching lines of poems. Bivalve shells were used in particular for this pastime, because each half of such a shell can only be perfectly paired with the other. Due to the perfect match between the halves of this shell, *kai-awase* came to be seen as a symbol of marriage vows. The containers for these shells were also painted or gold-lacquered, and a *kai-awase* set was typically included in a noblewoman's trousseau. Lovebirds, the typical motif on *kai-oke* containers, are also the symbol of happy marriage.

楽器文様

Musical instruments pattern

がつき

元来、楽器は神仏を荘厳する儀礼用具の鳴り物として、また奏上する囃し物として芸能用具から発達したもの。そんな楽器に節と言葉をつけて自分達の慰みとした楽しみの楽器も現れてきた。皆それらは大きく美しい音を出して鳴り響くことから、「成る」の意にかけて、五穀豊穣や祈願成就を表して楽器文様が描かれてきた。鼓、琴、笙、笛、鈴と数多い楽器の中から、よく好まれたのは王朝の黄鐘調を奏でた琵琶や琴、笙、笛の楽器であった。

Musical instruments were originally used in ceremonies to honor Shinto and Buddhist deities. It was only later that people began to play music for entertainment. As musical instruments produce the purest of tones, they came to symbolize all that was ideal: hopes for a bountiful harvest, or any wish fulfilled; as such, these idealized images began to be seen in various kimono patterns. Hand drums, Japanese harps, Shinto flutes, bamboo flutes, and bells were used to play traditional Japanese music, but some instruments were used specifically to play Imperial melodies: the harps and flutes mentioned above, in addition to Japanese lutes; this latter group provided the most popular images in kimono patterns.

花篭図は中国の八仙人の一人である
藍采和の持ち物として瑞祥文様とされ
ている。それを長柄の車に乗せて花車
図が江戸初期の狩野派によって描かれ
た。その典拠は室町時代に描かれた
移春檻図という名花銘木を車に乗せて
描いた絵によるといわれる。近代以降、
王朝への憧れも手伝って広く用いられ、
婚礼衣装の打掛けなどに豪華に描か
れた。

Kano school painters would portray
images of flower carts in the early Edo
period. This pattern was an extension
of the flower basket, a motif that
appeared in Chinese paintings
depicting one of the eight hermits,
Ransaiwa, known as the carrier of the
flower basket. The source image for the
flower cart design is believed to be
another work of art entitled *Ishunkan-
zu*, drawn in the Muromachi period. In
modern times, this pattern has been
widely employed in gorgeous wedding
kimono, due in part to the sense of
ceremony associated with this design.

花車文様

Flower cart pattern

はなぐるま

手毬文様

Temari pattern

てまり

手毬も初めは、今の私達が球技に使うようなよく弾む毬ではなかった。木綿が利用されるようになって、綿を芯にして表面を美しい色糸で飾った弾む「手毬」ができた。一方、弾む鞠は「蹴鞠」などに使われた革製の鞠で、足で蹴り合って公家の遊戯として用いられたもの。どちらも文様によく見られるが、手毬は女児の玩具ばかりでなく、五色の糸かがりで美しい文様を見せて装飾品としても愛され、文様に最適だった。今も日本中に伝えられている。

Early *temari* (a traditional handball) were not bouncy like those we see today. These balls only began to bounce when people started to use cotton as the *temari*'s core material, decorating its surface with colorful decorative threads. On the other hand, the bouncy *kemari* (a traditional soccer ball) was made of leather, and used by court nobles to play traditional football. *Temari* and *kemari* are popular kimono patterns, but *temari* were singled out for representation not only as a girl's toy but also as ornamental objects due to the attractive five-colored threads–a particularly suitable motif for kimono patterns.

折鶴文様

Origami crane pattern

おりづる

折り紙の起源は、日本や中国、果てまたスペインなどと言われて明らかでない。しかし、日本の「おりがみ」が世界の共通語として現在使われているのは「折り鶴」を代表して繊細で精緻な折り紙細工が、日本の他に勝ることのないからだろう。日本の折り紙で、代表ともいえる折り鶴を確認するのは江戸時代。井原西鶴の『好色一代男』に折り紙の比翼の鶴が記されるのが最初。また中期には伊勢桑名の魯縞庵義道が『秘傳千羽鶴折形』を図解して、49種の連鶴の折り方があった。

Various stories tell different tales of the origin of origami. Some say the craft originated in Japan; some say China; others say origami came from Spain. Regardless of origin, Japanese origami, including the celebrated "origami crane," is so elaborate that the Japanese word "origami" became the universal term to represent this particular paper craft. The first recorded origami cranes can be found in the literary work entitled *Koshoku Ichidai Otoko* written by *Saikaku Ihara*, dating back to the Edo period. The book entitled *Hiden Senbazuru Orikata* ("Linked Cranes from a Single Sheet of Paper"), written by *Rokoangido* in the mid-Edo period, illustrates 49 different origami cranes.

鳳凰文様

Phoenix pattern

ほうおう

中国から伝わる架空の動物として代表
的なものに龍と並んで鳳凰がある。鳳
凰は龍の一種である飛龍から鳥の祖と
して現れ、この鳳凰があらゆる鳥を生
んだという。鳳凰は天に棲む鳥で天帝
の使いとされ、前身が麟、後身が鹿、
首が蛇、尾は魚、鱗は龍、背は亀、顎
は燕、喙は鶏で、五色の羽根を有し、
五音で鳴くとされた。平和の善政を執
る聖徳の天子のもとには、鳳凰が地上
へ舞い降りて祝福するという。そんな
善政君主を徴し、中世期には桐竹鳳凰
文を天皇御衣の織紋に採用した。

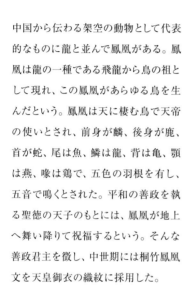

A phoenix is a representative example
of China's array of fabulous creatures,
standing alongside the dragon. It is said
that the phoenix was born from a *hiryu*
dragon, to become an ancestral bird
that would then give birth to a
multitude of avian species. The phoenix
is considered to be a servant of the
Emperor of Heaven. This creature is
believed to resemble the imaginary
qilin from the front but to appear as a
deer from the back; it has the neck of a
snake, a fish's tail, a dragon's scales, the
back of a tortoise, and bird's beak in
addition to feathers in five colors and
five different voices. Legend has it that
a phoenix once swooped down from
the heavens to honor a particularly wise
ruler. Based on this story, the phoenix
came to symbolize a peaceful reign. A
pattern of phoenixes, in combination
with depictions of paulownia and
bamboo plants, was woven into the
emperor's clothes in the Middle Ages.

花尽し文様

Hana-zukushi pattern

はなづくし

同じ目的や分類で括って取り揃えた文様を「尽し」という。数多くの物を集めて世に満たした富貴な吉祥を寿いでいる。そんな現世利益的なめでたさに浸り、あらゆる花々を一処に集めた花尽し文様がある。季節や約束事を気にせずに見た目に美しく並べるのが近代の花尽し文様で、伝統の和花と新奇の洋花を混ぜて隙間なく詰めて飾った。花尽し文様はその華やかさと豪華さが身上で、位負けをせずに着こなせたのも子供の特権である。

The suffix "zukushi" is attached to names for patterns comprised of multiple repeating motifs. For example, the *hana-zukushi* pattern is an ample collection of various flowers in a repeating pattern, and is considered to be an auspicious design. The modern *hana-zukushi* pattern is filled with a lovely array of flowers, in depictions not limited based on season, native environment, or tradition. This pattern is so bright and gorgeous that only children can wear them; most adults find the design almost too splendorous.

弓岡勝美プロフィール

フリーのヘアー＆メイクアップアーティストとして活動していたのち現株式会社弓岡オフィスを設立、主宰となる。以後、雑誌、写真集やCDジャケット、CMなどの媒体を中心として活動する。又、着物の着付け・コーディネートなども手掛け、雑誌や写真集、CM、ドラマなどで活躍すると同時に着物のコレクションをはじめ、広告業界・雑誌業界・タレント業界向けに着物のレンタルを始める。

その後着物アンティークショップ「壱の蔵」を原宿に開く。以後、アンティーク着物ムーブメントの中心として精力的に活動を展開し、銀座松屋、横浜そごう、うめだ阪急などの百貨店催事にも参加。一方、古裂を使った押し絵やパッチワークなどの細工物も制作し展覧会を開催。その作風は上品で愛らしくファンも多い。主な著書『着物のお洒落自由自在アンティーク着物』（世界文化社2002年）、『昔きもののレッスン十二か月』（平凡社2003年）、『アンティーク振袖』（世界文化社2004年）、『きもの文様図鑑』（平凡社2005年）、『着物と日本の色』（ピエ・ブックス2005年）、『着物と日本の色─夏篇』『千社礼』（ピエ・ブックス2006年）、『おさんぽ着』（世界文化社2006年）。

Katsumi Yumioka Profile

Yumioka started his career as a freelance hair and make-up artist. His work soon extended in to the world of magazine, CD cover jackets, TV Commercial and more. He also worked his way in to the world of Kimono styling, where he soon started collecting antique kimono.

Eventually,Yumioka's collection developed into his kimono antique shop, Ichinokura. Active as an instigator of the Japanese antique Kimono movement, he has vigorously expanded his work, including exhibitions held at the Ginza Matsuya, Yokohama Sogo, and Umeda Hankyu department stores. He is also famous for his patchwork designs using old Japanese cloth. He has published many Kimono books for the Japanese market.

藤井健三

京都市立芸術大学卒。1972年から2004年まで京都市染織試験場に勤務し
（研究部長）、1986年から1994年まで色彩情報誌制作に携わる。現在、財
団法人西陣織物館顧問。日本の染織技術史、色彩、文様を研究。主な著
書は『京の色事典330』（平凡社2004年）、『織の四季京の365日』（佐藤
道子氏と共著、京都新聞出版センター2005年）など。

参考文献

長崎巌監修・弓岡勝美編『明治・大正・昭和に見る きもの文様図鑑』平凡社
喜多川守貞『近世風俗史』（『守貞謾稿』）岩波文庫
切畑 健『若草頌 子どもの衣装 田村コレクション』紫紅社
『別冊太陽 縮緬と古裂』平凡社
『着物の基本』アシェット婦人画報社
京都市染織試験場（現／京都市技術研究所繊維技術センター）『京都「花の色」』
京都市染織試験場（現／京都市技術研究所繊維技術センター）『京都「近代の色」』
尚学図書編『色の手帖』小学館
吉岡幸雄『日本の四季を彩る 和みの百色』PHP研究所
『眼で遊び、心で愛でる 日本の色』学習研究社
柳田國男監修・（財）民俗学研究所編『民俗学辞典』東京堂出版
大塚民俗学編『日本民族事典』弘文堂
三省堂編研究所『絵で見る冠婚葬祭事典』三省堂
文化出版局編『最新きもの用語辞典』文化出版局

着物と日本の色 子ども着物篇

Child Kimono and the colors of Japan
Kimono Collection of Katsumi Yumioka

編・コレクション	弓岡勝美
監修	藤井健三
着物撮影レイアウト	春日ノリヲ
ブックデザイン	石井佳奈　石田百合絵（ME & MIRACO）
撮影	奥山光洋（奥山写真事務所）
文	青木一平
イラスト	やまだやすこ
翻訳	白倉三紀子 / マクレリールーシー
翻訳監修	Tim Cohan
編集	関田理恵
発行人	三芳伸吾

2007年6月15日　初版第1刷発行

発行所	ピエ・ブックス
	〒170-0005 東京都豊島区南大塚2-32-4
	編集 Tel: 03-5395-4820　Fax: 03-5395-4821
	営業 Tel: 03-5395-4811　Fax: 03-5395-4812
	http://www.piebooks.com
	e-mail : editor@piebooks.com
	e-mail : sales@piebooks.com

印刷・製本	図書印刷株式会社

©2007 PIE BOOKS

Collection ©2007 Katsumi Yumioka / Ichinokura

ISBN978-4-89444-607-6　C0072

Printed in Japan